A Medicine Woman Speaks

An Exploration of Native American Spirituality

Cinnamon Moon

NEW PAGE BOOKS
A division of The Career Press, Inc.
Franklin Lakes, NJ

A MEDICINE WOMAN SPEAKS
Cover design by Lu Rossman
Typeset by Kristen Mohn
Printed in the U.S.A. by Book-mart Press

To order this title, please call toll-free 1-800-CAREER-1 (New Jersey and Canada:
201-848-0310) to order using VISA or MasterCard, or for further information on
books from Career Press.

The Career Press, Inc., 3 Tice Road, PO Box 687,
Franklin Lakes, NJ 07417
www.careerpress.com
www.newpagebooks.com

Library of Congress Cataloging-in-Publication Data

Cinnamon Moon.
    A medicine woman speaks : an exploration of Native American
spirituality / by Cinnamon Moon.
      p. cm.
    Includes bibliographical references and index.
    ISBN 1-56414-526-3 (pbk.)
      1. Shamanism--Miscellanea. 2. Indians of North America--Religion--
Miscellanea. I. Title.

BF1621 .C56 2001
299'.7—dc21

                            00-065377

DEDICATION

Dedicated to the loving memory of my father

ACKNOWLEDGMENTS

There are many individuals who have shared and given from their hearts to further the process of my enlightenment. I wish to extend my heartfelt appreciation to Mary Henderson, for opening my eyes and introducing me to the Lakota Medicine Path. Though she has dropped her robe, I honor her efforts. To Little White Chicken for her friendship, laughter, and sharing of the Medicine Path. To Loretta Saggert, who has also dropped her robe, for sharing the wisdom of her years, a very opinionated view of history, and her Medicine.

I wish to thank those who walk their talk with dedication and sharing. To Tinker and Advent for their deep and abiding friendship, sharing of spiritual wisdoms, teachings, and allowing me to grow with them in so many ways. To Wolfsong, ElfLuc, Nofi, Mariah4Winds, Dancing Fox, Lune, Northernwolf, Otter, all my friends at Spirit Lodge, and countless others too numerous to mention for your loving friendship, support, and invaluable encouragement. To Trish Telesco, who in warmth and friendship has assisted me in so many ways. Last but not least, to my family for all the joy and love you bring.

From my heart to yours, I thank you one and all.

With great love and many blessings,
Cinnamon Moon

A Prayer For All
Who Read These Pages

Spirit, hear my words. I ask that this body of work may introduce its readers to the elements of the Medicine Path. That its contents lift the Veil of Illusion that is the mundane, thus opening mind and heart to the realms of your Great Mystery. I ask that All Our Relations be witness to this prayer guiding my work with the blessings of the Four Winds and the Ancient Ones. May these pages contain only words of truth and enlightenment. May those who read those words be blessed as they ride the winds of spiritual freedom, dance amid the Rainbow People, and find peace upon their paths. May they embrace each day and receive its blessings as they learn to walk between the worlds and know the many ways of Great Mystery. May each heart come to see that we are all one and find the inner strength to be a warrior of peace, keeper of wisdom, and caretaker of Mother Earth. Ho!

—Cinnamon Moon

CONTENTS

Part 2: Wielding the Medicine

PREFACE

Come, take my arm and walk with me, let me share with you what it is to look through the eyes of a Medicine Woman. To help you understand this evolutionary process we step back in time. The year was 1952. At the age of 5 I had become seriously ill. A high fever drove me down into a deep sleep where the spirit of a shaman came to me. He said he was going to help take me back, because I did not belong there—a place not of this world, perhaps the realm of the dying. The trust and innocence of a small child allowed me to see his kind, gentle spirit and the truth in his eyes. Without fear I accepted the help he offered. Exuding the love of a grandfather with a twinkle in his eyes, he made me laugh as we played tag. He guided me back to the surface along a spinning spiral pathway. To this day I can still see him dancing along the vibrant red and white swirls, teasing me to the surface of the fever that had consumed me. His presence has been with me ever since, appearing in times of serious need to fulfill his role as my spiritual protector.

There was also the guardian spirit of Wolf that accompanied me in those days. She watched over me at night, standing in the dark shadows reassuringly. She would tell me things in a strange way, for she did not speak aloud but imparted her thoughts to my mind. I received the impression that I was a Witch. Few small children have any idea what that means and I was no different, so I became attracted to the stories of Witches whenever one was mentioned. Wolf told me to be a "good Witch," and I agreed, thinking it meant the same thing as being the "good girl" my grandmother always reminded me to be. I had no cultural background in the ways of Native Americans at that time, only insinuations from now-deceased relatives. This was probably the closest Wolf could come to impressing me with the perception of being a Witch. It was the best way I could come to understand her message at that age.

Wolf kept her silent vigil with a dedication that nurtured a gentle strength, remaining with me throughout my adolescence. I accepted her presence as a natural part of my life. I cannot tell you for certain when she slipped into the background, other than it was about the time the innocence of childhood passed away and reality began to set in. One day she was just gone, and I was left with a lingering pang of sadness. She had done this at her own discretion, and I would later learn that this is often the way of our Animal Guides, who have their own will and know best when it is time to depart.

During my early to mid-teens I was experiencing things Otherworldly. Gifts began to surface that I did not understand. I chose to remain silent about them. After all, how do you tell someone that time stops or slows its motion so you can see deeply into the moment? How do you explain your spirit pulling away from your body when you cannot understand it yourself? But I found solace when I recalled the teachings of Wolf and decided that these gifts were part of what a "Witch" was. I struggled, and learned to depend on my inner spirit for guidance.

At night I would slip into a gray void where I was safe. It felt as if I was in the belly of Wolf and secure. I began to recognize a ringing in my ears signaling that a message was coming to me from Spirit and it was time to look for signs. Though I had no idea back then who was sending these messages to me, I had grown accustomed to Wolf's teachings, assuming they were from the spirit realms. I suddenly knew things I could not explain but accepted as truths. I did not know how to express that I recognized places I had never visited, knew the nature of a room I entered for the first time, or the emotions and heart of a stranger. I could not explain how I looked into someone's eyes to see the truth within him or know her intentions. How can you tell someone that you know these things when there is no rational explanation for the information? How do you explain that you see energy flowing like a river, or the bright lights of spirits hovering in the air? How do you express clouds showing you things coming to pass, or that you see halos around people, plants, and landscapes? I was certain that anyone who may have found out about my abilities would think I had completely lost my mind.

Through trial and error I learned many things about my strange and often frightening gifts. As they emerged, sometimes slowly and at other times quite spontaneously, I adapted accepting them as a natural process of life, albeit a secretive one. I saw nothing evil or wicked about the gifts that would come from my intentions. Nor did I see anything wicked in how I used them. Something told me that if they were abused they would be lost to me, and I did not want that to happen.

As I honed my skills, I began to understand them better. If they frightened me too much, I would shove them away in a dark corner of my being and pretend they did not exist. This created blockages, which I had to struggle through for a long time in order to revive my abilities. I now had to exert much more effort in learning to wield them again. It was all part of the trials of self-teaching. That took place in the late 1950s and early 1960s. Today I have no trouble saying I have a number of Totem Animals and Spirit Guides that work with me as allies, teachers, and guardians. I honor them. Nor do I have trouble openly using the Gifts of Spirit that took years to hone and master.

The road that brought me here was a long and often lonely one. I was raised in a fairly permissive atmosphere, being allowed to explore religion, philosophy, and metaphysics openly while growing up. As a result, my spiritual upbringing seemed quite natural. My family was Lutheran and I was confirmed in that faith at the age of 13. My great aunt was Pentecostal. Her beliefs were fundamentally stricter than the Lutheran Church I attended. Her behavior was dictated by definite rules of conduct that were not like the ones I was raised by. I was a thorn in her side more often than not, so she imparted guilt and fear as a means of control. I began to see differences in what a Christian was and it really bothered me. There were many questions on my mind in those days, and the answers that came left me feeling unfulfilled. I think I was the most difficult student that my minister had encountered. Stopping by his office all the time seeking answers he found challenging to explain, I exasperated him. He tried very hard to be patient, doing the best he could to satisfy a young girl's mind.

Why did I need to fear God? Why did I need to bear the guilt of sins my ancestors committed? Would I really burn in Hell for the emerging talents I was experiencing and unable to deny? Was this what religion was all about, or was there more? Why could I not just have a one-on-one relationship with God? Did I need the Church to tell me what I could or could not believe? If so, how could I stop believing in what I knew to be true from the experiences I was encountering surrounding the manifestations of my abilities? Why did the majority of these things that were happening to me not show in the Lutheran teachings? Of those that did, why were they said to be evil? I had lots of questions.

At that age I had realized I needed to seek my own answers. I did not completely turn my back on the Church, but other directions were calling. I knew that I was a bit of a rebel, but at the core of my being I knew there was magick in the world and that it was not evil in and of itself. Somehow I knew evil came from the intentions of the practitioner. It only made sense. In addition, I knew that Christianity was not telling me all I was sure I could discover, and I knew the Church frowned deeply on people like me. I was a Witch and I knew it. People did not like Witches. It was black and white back then, and I felt life had forced me to cross over a line. There was a gradual pulling away. I often skipped church to go for walks in the park or bird sanctuary. Enhancing what I had learned in Christianity, I became aware of my inner spirit in ways I had never anticipated. Enlightenment was sporadic and often brought with it an "Ahhh Ha!" or hushed "Wow" of amazement. I was left with experiences that I had never found within the Lutheran Church and a longing to explore them deeper.

My father was the most wonderful, loving man I have known. He was an Elder in the Church, and would have nothing to do with my own beliefs (or "witcheries," as he called them). Still, we loved one another deeply, and respected each other's right to choose their path. He was a gentle soul who taught me many things, the greatest of which was that I should perceive life through love and respect. He demonstrated that despite the path others may choose to take, we all have our lessons to learn. He taught me that each of us is entitled to his or her own views and should not force them upon anyone, that by respecting the views of others I could often learn a great deal. He taught me to reason why I should or should not act in given situations. I never once recall him bringing a tear to my eye or making me feel less of a person for my beliefs. Instead, my memories are of a wise and loving man who encouraged me to be the best I could be.

My mother was strict, and often our views about how one should live clashed. On many occasions, she was controlling and distant. Her stringent ways drove a wedge between us. It was one that continued to expand as I grew more independent. There was one area, however, that we could communicate on.

Mother was a student of the paranormal and occult. It was not uncommon to see her sitting with the Ouija board in her lap or her nose buried in a book on the supernatural. Her love of the strange and unusual left room to investigate many topics and is perhaps behind my own love for unique things to this day. She openly shared her views and interests with me well into the late night hours on endless occasions.

My maternal grandmother attended séances, but because she was a devout Lutheran, her indiscretions were kept as a family secret. Now and then she would speak of her experiences, but always in a whisper. Grandmother, along with my great aunt (affectionately known as Nanny) who lived with us, heavily influenced my character by teaching me right from wrong in gentle ways. They taught me to be a lady and to speak properly. They also taught me that the value of my opinions mattered. In this I learned the wisdom of theirs, to respect my Elders, and listen to their stories beyond the tellings to the deeper meanings they held.

It was my grandmother who taught me how to give. She would do something I felt needed repaying and when I tried, she told me to "pass it on" to someone else instead. I thought that was a beautiful thing to do and a lesson I never forgot. Through Nanny I learned that love is forgiveness and the ability to say you are sorry for hurting someone. She showed me how to use my imagination and create worlds of my own. With the influence of three strong-minded women I grew to appreciate the nurturing love they provided. They did not judge me for my mistakes; instead I was taught to learn from them and to grow wiser by not repeating them. They taught me how to cope with my humanity by using humble methods of learning from my faux pas when I repeated them, and having a sense of humor about it.

After my parents divorced my mother met and married a kind, gentle man who was a Bohemian gypsy. Among other things, my stepfather was telepathic. Things moved in his presence, spirits seemed to follow him around, and he was able to start fires from a distance of at least 20 feet. He demonstrated his gifts openly to the family, but did not believe they

were to be presented in public. He insisted on that, and impressed me
with the respect he held for his ways. He claimed the world was not ready
for the responsibility that knowledge required. Coming from a strong
family tradition, he could see no other way than to guard his gifts to avoid
placing his knowledge in careless hands.

The gypsy beliefs seemed to be further strengthened by the books I
was reading about Witchcraft. Those books repeatedly stated that the
teachings were to be kept secret, away from those who did not understand them or would abuse the knowledge. Today I know that school of
thought was a product of the times. It would not be for at least another
decade or so that the Native Americans would reclaim their rights to
their religion or that Witchcraft would become legal and accepted in the
United States.

Mother remained a student, choosing instead to dabble here and
there with things that held her interest for a time, but she never became
a practitioner. She liked the pendulum and Ouija, going to palm readers,
tea rooms, and card readings, but she chose instead to leave the skills to
others and live vicariously through the gifts my stepfather held. It was
shortly before she dropped her robe (leaving her physical body behind in
death) that she expressed her regrets in not taking her exploration of
spirituality further and wanting to do that soon. She told me she wanted
to know more about my path, but her time was short at that point and the
teachings were not hers to acquire. It was a lesson for me as well. I realized once again how true it is that we need to make the most of each day
we are given. We need to honor Spirit in our lives in order to grow, or we
become stagnated.

Those who influenced me in my early years have all passed over into
Spirit, but the love they gave and the lessons they taught remain. My
family was tolerant of the ways of others and I enjoyed my ability to
peruse these paths as a very normal part of life. I had no idea back then
this was all that unusual until I stepped out into the world a bit more. In
my late teens I was well into the study of the occult, paranormal, Witchcraft, and Spiritualism. I discovered the tarot and an innate ability to
read them with a high rate of accuracy, which led me to other methods of
divination. People were drawn to knowing the mysteries of life, and my
circle of friends began to shift as word got out that I did readings.

I possessed what was to become an insatiable thirst for folklore,
mythology, the occult, and Witchcraft, so I read everything I could get
my hands on over the years. Back in the late 1960s and early 1970s, books

on these subjects were not as prevalent as they are today. The good ones were rare, if not out of print, forcing me to haunt odd bookstores, order through the mail, and receive packages in plain brown wrappers.

At 20 I began attending a Spiritualist Church in the hope of finding a clearer pathway. Participating in séances, mastering meditation, and continuing to search for answers, Spiritualism was interesting. The Spirit Guides I knew were accepted, and communication with them was seen as a sacred act. As it turned out I was to uncover fraud and deception. It was so disheartening to discover that a man who took the role of a servant to God was misleading his congregation. I quickly learned all is not what it seems—I take nothing for granted, and question all that others profess to teach me.

I am not saying that all Spiritualist Churches are like the one I just described, but this particular minister was a scam artist. I caught him in the act of falsifying both the séances and apport sessions. Furious, I told him why I was leaving, that he was no more than a stage magician, and a poor one at that. Having been betrayed by this individual, the experience was very personal. I look back on it now realizing I should have exposed him openly. But I was young and shy, so regretfully it was not the case; I had expended much of my courage confronting him, and instead I just walked away.

Understanding the need for tolerance, I had come to a point where once again my path took me along other roads and away from organized religion. Instead I turned to the Old Religion and became immersed in the teachings of Witchcraft, reading books, taking correspondence courses through the mail, and practicing the arts of the Craft. It was fulfilling in ways, but the rituals and spells were not what I was looking for; I needed more, or at least something different. I was still seeking to find myself, to understand the spirituality of the magickal realms, as well as my path. I did not want to control or manipulate anyone, and my use of spells was primarily for healings or visions. The road was about to fork once again.

I was reunited with an old schoolmate at that time, a Lakota woman named Mary, who opened my eyes to many things. The ways of the Native Americans, their spirituality, customs, and insights about life had sparked an interest. As we shared our views we found many similarities, and much of what I had experienced on my own began to make more sense. Mary's ways intrigued me, as did her willingness to spend endless hours sharing her knowledge. What began to emerge in me was a growing passion for spirituality. I loved the myths, legends, and stories she told. Over the years I came to feel it was much more a part of me than anything else I had come to know. Mary did not discriminate against me because I was a white woman; instead she encouraged me to discover more. In her I saw a fire, a passion for life, and a gentle sharing spirit.

In the early 1980s, Mary needed a pacemaker because her heart was giving her a lot of trouble. The alcohol she consumed had taken its toll and her body cried out. The first operation was a disaster and a second one was to follow. While she was in the hospital's intensive care unit recovering, she had an unusual experience. Looking up from her bed she saw an Indian Chief standing outside the window of her room. He was dressed in buckskins, wearing a full eagle-feather headdress, and he was smiling. Mary was weak, and she fell asleep shortly after seeing him. When she awoke it was to discover a mark on her breast that formed a perfect pair of lips. It made no sense to her, and she began to ask questions.

When the nurses came in she asked about the man, but no one had seen him or knew how the mark appeared on her breast. It was not until her mother arrived that Mary would learn what it meant. Through tears, her mother explained that it had been a Spirit Chief who had visited her, given her the Kiss of Death, and there was cause for concern. If she was not careful her days would be numbered. We talked about the incident many times over the next few months, but Mary was unable to conquer her need for alcohol. She dropped her robe, passing over into Spirit less than six months after the operation.

I will always be grateful for the gift she gave me as well as the treasure-trove of love and wisdom it contained. We shared teachings for 13 years and at 34, my dear friend went down an old path. She had impressed upon me all she could, teaching me to see through new eyes the poetry of her people. I felt I had finally come home when just before her death she made me promise to read the book *Seven Arrows* by Hyemeyosts Storm. She told me it would help me along the path I was being called to follow. I kept that promise, and in doing so began a quest to find out more about this spiritual pathway. I vowed to her that when Spirit sent signs I would heed them.

One book led to another, and I discovered more of the teachings and the ways of the Medicine Men. They integrated quite naturally with what had already become my own spiritual views. In my early thirties I returned to college, satisfying a growing need to understand more about life. I attained minors in philosophy, sociology, psychology, and creative writing. I studied comparative religions and gathered more along the lines of folklore and mythology through independent studies. All these areas added to my perceptions of the world feeding my eclecticism.

Shortly after that I was to meet another Native American woman, Little White Chicken, who to this day is a very dear friend. She has shared with me her love, laughter, and heritage. Being of mixed blood, her teachings included those of the Delaware Tribe of Oklahoma, and the Cherokee. Her mother, Loretta, became a friend and mentor, sharing years of wisdom and women's Medicine with me before passing into Spirit herself. Loretta's passing put a book, *Oklahoma Delaware Ceremonies, Feasts and Dances by the American Philosophical Society in Philadelphia*, into the hands of Little White Chicken. The book, which was published in 1937, proved to be a rare and out-of-print copy detailing the many ceremonies, songs, and rituals of the Delaware. She brought it to my attention and urged me to study it. Again I had been gifted with a sharing that went beyond what I had expected. She also found a book in her mother's things listing many of the herbal remedies used by her people. This she gifted me with.

These women shared, in such generous ways, not only their wisdom, but their crazy stories and their song of laughter. They touched the spirit within and taught me the meaning of Aindahing (home within the heart where the Great Mystery dwells and we are all One). Through Little White Chicken and Loretta I met two Medicine Men who were more than willing to answer my questions and help guide me. In the years that have followed, I have known an Apache Medicine Woman and other friends of Cherokee blood. It was the wisdom of these warm and loving people that was highly influential in stirring within me a deep love for the Medicine traditions.

Through their openness I began to see that things sacred and secret could be shared with those who were sincere, and it was along this path I found my true calling. Today I am a Medicine Woman, an ordained minister, and it is from my heart that I am dedicated to the teachings where cultures and races are embraced rather than becoming issues of division. I know by allowing people to grow together in the love and enlightenment of Spirit, we can touch lives and evolve in wondrous ways. Highly eclectic in nature, I strive to create the ground on which the Rainbow People (people of all races and faiths) can come together as one to teach and learn. I have recognized that the unseen hands of Spirit lead us to doors and people who are instrumental to our paths.

As a Medicine Woman I have assisted many in their spiritual quests. My research and studies continue, and I deeply enjoy learning, growing, and sharing with others. There is a basic common ground running through all cultures, systems of magick, views of spirituality, and religions. That link is shamanism, a term that stems from Slavonic and Siberian origins now spilled over into our society. Today it is an almost generic expression for one who walks the Medicine Paths in any culture. Every path has its own Medicine. The truth of the matter is that shamanism presents an accessible route to finding the answers for spiritual questions. I have found my way and a place in life where I can continue to learn and contribute to the growth of others as well.

For more than 35 years, I have taught these methods to family members and those who have come seeking to know. In this process I have seen a need, a hunger for a better understanding of the Medicine Paths. My studies have included more than 8,000 miles of travel, first-hand experiences at sacred sites throughout the United States, visiting ruins of various cultures throughout the Americas, work with Ley Lines and vortexes, and touching the face of the Spirit of Place residing in many different locations. I walk between the worlds, have come to know the elemental forces of nature and spirits, the Voice of the Land, animal spirits, guides, and most of all Spirit. Through my love for Great Mystery and in answering the call sent to me, the experiences of vision quests, shamanic journeys, and the channeling of Source Energy flowing through the Web of Life have been gifted to me.

PART 1

FUNDAMENTALS
OF THE
MEDICINE PATH

CHAPTER 1

INTRODUCTION:
PART 1

The making of a Medicine Woman does not just happen. It is a process of evolution, of traveling down a road with many forks through decades of experience, and it is that experience that transforms the individual over time. It is a world of deep spiritual insight containing elements of cultural influences steeped in tradition and personal Medicine. There have been many books written about the Medicine Path based on anthropological studies and scholastic views. This is not one of them. While those books have their place, the views of the practitioner need expression to help define personal experiences, shamanic realities, and balance the perspectives between the literary scholar and actual practitioner. Expression is needed through exploring deeper and sharing with others who understand these things. It means having a comfort zone to acknowledge the experience in detail. The choice of that expression is up to the individual. Such spiritual experiences beg to be honored and they have a lesson that is a gift, one that is shared and so continues to give. The expression does, however, command a select audience. Not everyone can accept these events as reality.

Firsthand knowledge has value, and a view from the inside is a bit different. My teachings are a combination of the feminine and masculine perspectives from those who have shared their wisdom and my path for a time. My road was not limited to a narrow horizon.

If you are just starting out on this path looking for power through spells and have come here to find it, you are looking in the wrong place. I have taught for many years, and the last thing on my list is teaching spells. That is not how it begins. This is first a path of spirituality, which should be foremost in your mind. If that is not the case, then you are walking a path I do not instruct on. It is necessary to have a sound foundational understanding of the forces and the spirits you will be working with.

It is important to know what spirits you want to invoke—to know who or what they are when they show themselves. It is important to know they will challenge you. They are not puppets. Consider these things, and in that consideration build upon a fundamental structure so you can gain internal strength in the process. You need to know what to do if the results of an action go chaotic and how to stop it. You cannot just whip out a spell, have it go wrong, then turn your back on it or start shouting for help. It just does not work that way. Knowing what to do before those things happen, understanding when and why ritual and ceremonies take place, and forming the foundation of the path you walk is imperative. This is not a playground.

Do not just ask anyone for his or her Medicine. Although most people are very good souls, you should really get to know them, have a sound grasp of their integrity, and understand their values. Know why you want to weave magick, and understand that you are probably going to get exactly what you ask for. If someone is willing to hand you information blindly, I would really question her reason for doing so. Does she want you to become dependent upon her? It is a given that they are acting carelessly and recklessly. Facing facts, there are those who simply do not care what happens. Do not trust your education or acquisitions to them. Always be aware of gifts offered freely by those you do not know, and the hidden price tags they have in their pockets.

My words come from decades of practical experience and I would never ask for, nor accept, Medicine from someone I did not know extremely well and have the utmost respect for. Even then, I would tear it apart piece by piece, examine it closely, and reassemble it in the ways I know to be proper. Please do not ever work blindly. Consider these words as those of caution for your best interests. They are not a condemnation of your eagerness. That I admire. I would hope you will direct it properly because there are no shortcuts on the Medicine Paths, and each lesson has its price. If you cheat, you will cheat yourself. So begin on the right foot to walk the path before you.

Entering upon any path is not something that is done lightly. One does not just jump in here or there and select what he wants to learn and expect to be good at what he does. To start at the beginning and go from there requires a lot of reading, learning about histories, traditions, philosophies, and more. This body of work is designed to show how the fundamentals build the structure of what you are developing for yourself. Anything less is dishonoring the ethics of the path you walk.

Eagerness is all well and good, but learning to stand on your own so you can become stronger is better. Look closely at the books you read and remember they are, at best, only presented from the views of the author. Know your reasons for being attracted to a path. It is not entertainment, and there are a great many risks to the inexperienced practitioner, so do not fool yourself into believing otherwise. Some people might get away with reckless behavior on the surface, and it may appear to you to be a lucky thing for them. In truth, luck has nothing to do with it. All actions bring a reaction in one form or another, and you can bet your bottom dollar that the results of any given action will come back much stronger than they were intended, for better or for worse.

Be wise and learn more of the path you are investigating first. Then, when you are sure the path you have chosen is right for you, there will be ample time for wielding its Medicine. You will know what to ask, how to judge the path and be counted among the wise. Know what responsibility is and that if placed in the wrong hands you are just as much to blame as the individual to whom you give your Medicine. No one needs to suffer the consequences of stupidity. Take this to heart and let it guide you as you find your way.

Stand tall, walk proud, know your intentions, and maintain the highest standard of integrity you possibly can. That will help build your character and make you strong. These words are not intended to discourage you in your search for knowledge, but to encourage you to search in ways that will be to your greatest advantage. Learn to be the best you can be at what you do and to honor the pathway that you walk.

My knowledge and basis for practice are founded on eclectic lines, taking what worked for me specifically, and discarding what did not. I found my own way, discovering that the teacher does arrive when the student is ready. I have learned that opportunity will present itself repeatedly, that if one door does not open, another will. It is true that if we are dedicated, patient, and persevering we will come to find our way and the enlightenment that we seek. Through education, the generosity of friends, books, much trial and error, and my eclectic nature, I have come to my credentials such as they are. I do not claim academic expertise, but I do claim to know who and what I am as well as the path I walk.

Native American spirituality has brought me deeper into nature and the realms of Spirit than any path I have known. It has brought with it enlightenment and fulfillment, as well as a deep assurance that in truth We Are All One. I strongly believe that all Gods and Goddesses are One, that they are but aspects we perceive in our efforts to conceive the whole. In that union they combine to become Great Mystery, Spirit, the Creator, or the Powers That Be in whatever form you perceive them. Religious teachings are not compromised because of this. Anyone is free to expand and incorporate these ways into his or her spiritual growth. When we realize that life provides us with many teachers, and it is up to us to discern their truths, we gain a deep insight into the way that teachings take place. In following our own path we become free to express perceptions, not only in terms of a spiritual existence, but in terms of social acceptance as well. In this way we open our eyes and expand both the mind and inner spirit so we may evolve.

When the eyes are opened wide we begin to see our paths clearly before us. We seek the freedom to read, practice, learn, and grow. Reading what you will, working in areas that appeal to you, practicing and honing skills, and learning from those you come into contact with will create in you a spectacular individuality; it will create a persona that radiates your own soul-shine. It will allow you to be confident in all that you do, validating your path and setting you free. What is then presented here is an eclectic philosophy, some personal observations, truths I can share, and the results you can expect from working with them from a Medicine Woman's point of view.

Women's spirituality has its own aspects, and throughout the pages that follow it will be pointed out where it is appropriate. I present them alongside the teachings of the shaman as a woven tapestry whose strands come from ancient wisdoms, magickal lore, and personal experience, a tapestry that is fulfilling and rewarding for anyone who takes the time to examine it.

Throughout the centuries and lands, shamanic practices have taken place. They have been handed down orally through cultures, families, and groups that practice various traditions. These same practices have filtered into the melting pot of America, offering many traditions that bring a wealth of information and knowledge. It is in our nature to be eclectic souls in one way or another and draw from the sources around us. In this same context we can develop a style of spirituality and activities we find most compatible with our perceptions. This is what I have done and what I propose you can do as well no matter what religion you follow.

I invite you to continue to walk with me and explore the many fascinating aspects of a Medicine Woman's ways. There are vast horizons that will embrace your mind and spirit as we continue to progress through these teachings. Enlightenment awaits you. You will not become a Medicine Woman or shaman simply by reading this material, though it may transform your thinking in the course of expanding your visions. It offers the opportunity to decide for yourself what is right for you. Truths may be revealed to us at any given moment, but a book can only lead you to a door; you must choose to open it yourself, and experience your own gifts so you may know the mystery that life holds.

True learning comes from doing, and only you can decide who your teachers are to be, and when they have ceased to teach. Only you can decide when to reach out in a new direction. Guidance is always there if we learn to look for it, but it is only valid if we choose to apply it to our path. Be discerning and weigh the words that come to you, deciding for yourself if the Medicine Paths are calling to you to follow. Do this with namaji, with respect, honor, dignity, and pride. Do it with impeccable intentions. May you walk with Spirit on your journey through life.

CHAPTER 2

DEVELOPING a SPIRITUAL PHILOSOPHY

The philosophy of a spiritual path is unique to each individual. A central philosophy of Medicine Women and shaman's is found in the common belief that the energy of the Creator is manifest in Nature. If you can accept this premise and remain open to experiencing that manifestation, then you are well on the way to understanding the foundation of the Medicine Paths. Ultimately, what will be most important to you is to know and develop your own philosophy.

Through the basic Elements of Air, Fire, Water, and Earth, there exist parallel worlds of the mundane and Spirit. These worlds have multiple dimensions that are often described as the layers of an onion. It is through these layers (or veils) that the individual practitioner may experience the realms of Spirit coming to Oneness with the Creator or Great Mystery. The energy of life pulsates, spirals, cycles, and permeates throughout the universe, leaving nothing untouched. Like the wind of a silent storm, or the flow of a transparent river winding its way through all that exists, this philosophy allows us to learn ways of tapping what I call Source Energy. In tapping this energy and working with it I have come to know Great Mystery without the boundaries of time or space. Energy is unhampered by animate or inanimate objects and is both invisible as well as visible to the naked eye. It is perceived as it resides and expresses itself most readily in the manifestation of the elemental forces of Air, Fire, Water, and Earth.

Although we can physically experience the Elements, their counterparts within the spiritual realms are found within their respective dimensions, which are located in the sacred directions of the North, South, East, or West, and are present in a spiritual context. All things take form in the realms of Spirit before they can manifest in the physical world. This means that all creation, healing, Medicine, and magick must first exist through Spirit or the entities that serve it.

In the spirit realms dwell a variety of spiritual entities serving Great Mystery through the elemental forces and the laws that govern them. They aid the practitioner who honors them. Notice I did not say worships them. I am not telling anyone to bow down before a God, Goddess, or Deity of any sort. Honoring the pirits present, showing respect, and perhaps establishing a relationship with them is all that I am addressing. By honor I mean demonstrating personal integrity, and presenting ourselves with dignity. It is that simple, and it is impeccable. Such spiritual entities have many names, whether you call them Angels, Spirits, Totems, Protectors, Guides, Allies, or by some other term. They do exist, and they are just as real as we are.

To those of the Medicine Paths there are an additional three concepts of great importance: the Above World of the Star People, the Below World of the Ancestors, and the Middle World of the mundane and spiritual center. These Worlds, plus the four Elements and their directional dimensions, combine to form the Seven Sacred Directions. As a Medicine Woman I center myself amid the Seven Sacred Directions and become One with them. (These concepts are discussed in further detail in Chapter 12.) It is in this way that I walk between the Worlds. I see this center to be wherever I am at the moment and dwell within the Now, literally taking that center within the core of my being. It goes with me no matter where I am. The past lives in the Now, for it can be summoned from memory to the moment at hand. The future lives in the Now for it is the action of the moment that brings the future into being. The Now is complete.

Dwelling in this state at all times, the Medicine Path provides us with a direct link to Spirit. There are those who will use rituals, spells, incantations, and weavings to accomplish magickal results and direct the energy flows. The shaman, however, becomes the Element, the energy, the animal spirit, or the entity of choice and in that union shapeshifts to wield the energy directly with Spirit. The techniques of shamanism and Native American Medicine blend well with those of paganism and magick. To the shaman, Medicine is the true magick of the universe; it is the wielding and healing, the service of creating a balanced spiritual center for themselves, and for those they serve.

Witchcraft and paganism are shamanic in nature; however, shamanism is not Witchcraft. Both the Witch and the shaman know that intent (the purpose and reason behind an action) is key to success. They know that the work done is reflected back upon the doer because we are all a part of the greater whole. When the work is directed outward and a finger pointed in a direction, it must follow that there are three other fingers on that same hand pointing back at us. So the work that is done is best done for the benefit of Mother Earth and All Our Relations. Integrity, the value we place on our own morals and ethics along with what we are willing to do to uphold them, is of utmost importance. There is no room for selfishness, and in this the Witch and the shaman are the same.

They are also different in certain ways. The shaman walks at all times between the Worlds, seeing no lines of division between dimensions and physical reality, but rather a unified whole. The Witch does not. A Witch will enter the circle to draw upon these dimensional realms for a short span of time, more or less stepping in and out of them to work. When the work is completed, there is a return to the mundane world the shaman does not define. A shaman dwells in continual spiritual awareness, where the Witch needs to focus on it to summon that state of mind.

Keep in mind that since the beginning of time humanity has attempted to give Source Energy a name, a face, a persona that would allow the mind to comprehend its presence. So it is within the context of the world's religions that we are shown the many faces of the Gods and Goddesses as aspects of the Creator. This lacks a total perception. It is beyond human comprehension, and words do not come together to describe what is intangible. There are thousands of faces, thousands of names, pantheons and hierarchies of Gods, Goddesses, and multitudes of spiritual beings that serve them in a wide variety of ways. None of these concepts is wholly right or wrong, and each is to some degree incomplete, but they are the best we have for now.

Through our philosophies we can see the omnipotent force of the Creator take form as the duality of positive and negative images that balance one another. They are described as being masculine (positive) and feminine (negative). In this context, they are personified as God and Goddess energies that are in union with the whole of Spirit. Neither aspect of God or Goddess is complete without the other, and in this sense they are in truth One. Neither of them is truly a male or female being. They are androgynous energies, life forces that balance one and other to become the Creator.

Whatever religion or creation theory ascribed to will fit this model in some fashion. Through the many traditions of humanity we are able to recognize this duality. In doing so we are then able to honor all religions as being valid and worthy of tolerance. As individuals with strong eclectic natures, we can utilize the best each has to offer in ways that serve our personal needs. This gives us the freedom to explore the infinity of Spirit, to enter into the Oneness and hold to the Source of Life, for we are a part of it. We are each like a star in the night. As we gaze into the sky against the light of Grandmother Moon, we can see among their countless numbers that they are part of the fabric of life. They do not pretend to be more than they are, simply choosing to be is enough. We are gifted with their wisdom and each of us can emulate a star.

Long ago I realized that when we come to know our inner spirit, a transformation takes place. In that process we discover something marvelous. This spirit is the force within, set to guide and take us forward on a path of seeking true enlightenment. This is the true Self where our seat of power resides. It is our link to the Creator and the paths we follow. We are the sum total of our lives, past and present, as each of us has experienced events that color our perceptions to form our worldview. Despite whatever similarities may exist, we perceive through our eyes our own truths, coming to accept them and recognize their validity. Our eclectic natures, triggered by intuition, are the way our spirit teaches us to look here at this, and over there at that, to learn the lessons that are meant for us, not the person next door. In this same light it is our right to take these lessons, apply them to our lives, and live them. We are always in the process of Be Coming what we already are. In short, we create our own traditions from what we know, learn, and discover to be true and work best for us as individuals. Life is a banquet table spread with all the delicacies of the world and the desserts are sweet.

Incorporating the ideas and beliefs that work for you, in an eclectic fashion, will allow room for comparisons to be drawn and differences to be accepted, creating a harmonious blend and demonstrating a sense of balance in your way of doing things. Though your ways may be different from those of others, it is as it should be. Each of us is a unique creation of Spirit and in the end it is the journey we make that matters. How we carry ourselves defines our character, and we all end up in the arms of Spirit however that blessed presence is perceived.

Mystical, religious, or supernatural experiences touch each individual deeply in unique ways, allowing them to experience an undeniable truth. The Medicine Paths present us all with the opportunities to have just such experiences through shamanic trance, dreams, journeys, flight, shapeshifting, and vision quests. To others who may not be familiar with what these paths are, it is at best a possibility and at worst an insanity they may never come to understand. We must choose to walk our own path. Some people choose not to delve too deeply into spiritual matters or realms. That is okay, too. To say who is right regarding one's choice about their own reality and spirituality must come from the one who experiences the events. Those factors belong to those individuals and their reality becomes altered by a moment in and out of time. They may share a kinship with others who have experienced similar phenomena, but they will not be able to change their perception or share the event in the exact same way. They alone know what they saw, felt, or heard, unless that other person is a Medicine Woman or shaman experienced in journeying with others.

There will always be those who will not believe, or laugh at the mystery altogether, despite the fact that some may even have a form of tangible proof that an event took place. It is thus for each of us to decide what truths are to be accepted and not for others to dictate. The practices of the Medicine Path and one's spirituality are composed of many spiritual experiences. Much of what is learned is very often self-taught and gleaned along the way through trial and error. The practitioner learns from a variety of sources and applies this knowledge toward an ever advancing spiral of spiritual growth. At times there are various teachers who will cross paths with us, but the greatest of these is not of this world; it is that of Spirit. Embarking on these paths teaches us to come into contact with Spirit knowing that communion is possible, and to experience many things that others would classify as phenomena.

We are all the sum of our life experiences and environments. Why then should we not expect to reflect that in our spirituality? While religion is the worship of a Deity or pantheon, spirituality is a more personal path and one that we can each take control of as we see fit. Through the expression of ourselves we learn to strengthen our solitary ways. In my opinion, paganism, esoteric belief structures, and any religion incorporate well with the shamanic view. Shamanism breaks these concepts down into workable fractions. It does not claim that these fractions are all the Godhead, but portrays them as aspects of the whole as seen through nature. Seeing the Creator within all that exists, as a permeation of that life, is a shamanistic view. Through that you can create a spiritual tradition as unique as you are, with guidance from that same Creator. In the process of coming to discover your own identity and traditions, you will go through a wide variety of changes and down multiple roads. You must learn to harvest wisdom wherever it presents itself without prejudice. In the process you will discover inner harmony, residing peace, and a strong sense of balance. You will be content to have found your way to Spirit.

Without a doubt, I know and understand my own spiritual identity and feel very much at home with it. Can you say the same? If you are confused, searching, or troubled by your spiritual nature and are interested in a path that will serve you well, take the time to experience the Medicine teachings. There will be no tradition other than your own, no credo other than your own, only the freedom to follow a path that will certainly revolutionize your life. There is a freedom in exploring the wide variety of Native American cultural traditions. Such exploration allows a person to experience altered states of reality that exist in life. It permits individuals to formulate what is or is not going to work for them and in that, choose what will be accepted. Spirituality is not a religion. It does not demand traditional rules of conduct, but permits creativity and individualization/personalization of one's path. The tradition becomes yours, the freedom to follow a path of choice. While the Medicine Wheel, Spirits, and the Lines of Song are based on various traditions handed down over generations, they adapt to cultural or individual interpretations bringing an array of results and experiences relative to the interaction with them. I believe that all of life is magickal, that we are but the wielders, benders, and shapeshifters of our own energy and that which is borrowed from the Powers That Be. All Power belongs to Spirit.

At first you may feel like a closet nature spirit, but in time you will discover what it really means to touch the face of the Creator through your own perceptions. Through areas of the Medicine Path you will learn to combine these perceptions as the mysteries reveal the magick. To become a healer, lore keeper, seer, and enjoy a cosmic sense of humor is to know the Medicine. The eclectic path tends to be less cumbersome in today's world and is a path of wisdom in an arena in which you, too, may grow spiritually beyond your present aspirations. It allows you to work within the context of nature and the elements to serve the needs of humanity. Greatest of all it provides a venue to come to terms with your own spiritual self as never before.

A Good Teacher

In the course of eclectic study, you will have many sources of enlightenment and hopefully many teachers. Personally, I believe a good teacher is one who will guide you in your own discoveries; someone who will present to you truths, facts, methods, theories, and options that you can then apply and hone to fit your individual philosophy as it grows and develops maturity. I strongly feel that it is impossible for anyone to know all and be all wise, or any path to be the only one for that matter. Therefore, please be cautious of anyone who claims to have exclusive knowledge or power in any form. Be doubly cautious of those who ask for money for their teachings. If you are a mail-order student, materials may need to be purchased and mailing expenses covered, but these should be the most basic fees and not outrageous. The teachings of Spirit should not come with a "suggested retail price" when you are in a private teaching session, and anyone who asks absorbent fees should be weighed very cautiously.

Follow your own nature as it leads you to seek answers, trusting in your own body of knowledge and wisdom. It is meant to be shared with others, but not carelessly. In essence we are all students and teachers. Good teachers will share their personal wisdoms and truths, knowing when to send the student along to the next classroom. They are aware of the fact that they are not all wise and answers run out, and that resources can be exhausted. There are times this teacher-student relationship lasts no more than a few minutes and others when it can last for years.

A Good Student

As a good student you must trust your own instincts and know when the teacher has ceased to teach. A wise student will question the prospective teacher, get to know the person, and learn what he or she is about—their traditions, views, and opinions. This will often reveal areas that you are able to hold in high regard. When you respect them and their abilities, ask that they share their knowledge on an intimate level. Invariably you will learn as much or more in this manner than you will in any book or classroom. The one-on-one interaction allows for a greater depth of understanding and the ability to fine tune the skills you are receiving. You can take Shamanism 101 in many places. There are courses taught over the Internet, by mail, through books, and at local universities. However, with a basic understanding of the fundamentals, there does come a time for private lessons.

Keeping your mind and senses open allows you to broaden your horizons. Avoid the narrow-minded ways that exist and become a sponge...a very dry sponge. Learn to shapeshift into knowledge. The mundane world and those who walk within it can teach us much, but there is just as much to be learned from nature and the realms of Spirit, if not more. True learning comes through doing.

The Questions

A good teacher does not need to seek students, but watches and recognizes those who ask the right questions. Then, and only then, do they guide the student to their answers. What are the right questions? They are the sincere ones such as: "How do I find what I ache for deep within myself?" "What must I risk to achieve my freedom?" "What must I work for to achieve reaching my center?" "How can I overcome my fear that will not let me move forward?" "Can you teach me how to be true to my own spiritual needs?" "Can you teach me to be alone with myself, to love who I am?" These are questions a teacher will listen to, and they will ask questions of you as well. Questions like: "Will you study those things that seem insignificant but enlighten you?" "Are you willing to give up what you once were to Be Come who you already are?" "Are you living a life that is full and do you walk the path of the spiritual warrior?"

These, and questions like them, are the ones we must all ask ourselves as well. We must ask them from our cores. When we are faced with our blockages and obstacles (usually of our own making), we must learn to challenge ourselves to face our fears in the process. They are the questions the teacher is waiting to hear and the efforts that same teacher is waiting to see. A good teacher will help you see your way, help you to discover for yourself the fruits of your efforts, and develop your spiritual philosophy in your own way and time frame.

Spiritual Classrooms

My skills were honed to the greatest degrees within the Medicine Wheel and through interaction with the entities and spirits I have come to know. They were gleaned through ritual, in the Dream Lodge, in vision questing, meditation, and going within. Basics can be taught to anyone, but beyond this it is what you do with the skills that leads to greater knowledge and wisdom. Beyond the basic principles, beyond the theories and methods, there is only experience. Experiencing the dimensions of the many worlds allows for each of us to come to our own conclusions and realities. Seek experience and you will find knowledge, and through knowledge you will find wisdom.

On Being a Medicine Woman

A friend asked me once what the purpose was behind being a Medicine Woman. I explained to her that a Medicine Woman not only dances the Medicine Wheel, but also continues through that to enter into the shamanic journey (similar to astral projection) and work in the realm of Spirit. She knows what is there, that all things must take form in Spirit before they can manifest in the mundane. There are other paths that know these things but do not act on them as deeply. Instead, spells are cast and the Powers That Be are asked to perform the tasks that will bring about the results. As a Medicine Woman I am a doer; I take it upon myself to be responsible for all my actions. It is different for each of us, for we have our own unique Medicines. We may share them with others in that there are those who have the same gifts, but what we do with them and how we wield them is for each of us to determine. That is who we are, how we walk our Earth-walk, how we live our lives. It is what we intend to do in the service of Spirit, of Mother Earth, of humanity, and of All Our Relations. So it is for each of us to determine our way, purpose, and service.

A Call to Answer

We are called, shown, and asked to make a choice to do certain things. In that process we will then choose to either ignore or answer that call. It is a call that requires us to act on issues, become involved in certain things that we often would not have normally elected to act upon. It is the Will of Spirit that speaks to us and we have learned to listen to our inner spirit in answering our call. There is a compulsion to act. In learning to trust Spirit to guide us, the work gets done. That is what being a Medicine Woman is all about—the doing while walking with Spirit.

I knew many years ago that as part of my calling, I was to be a bridge for others who were finding their way. I was told I would guide some to enlightenment, and still others to places befitting their needs, all the while keeping Spirit in mind. Certainly I am not the only one to have received this call; I am one of many. For a long while I was waiting for the call to happen, like the striking of an anvil that would sound loudly that the time had come. As time passed I realized it was the path I was walking all along, and it had been happening quite naturally. There was no crusade, no massive movement, no huge battle to fight. Today that path is even clearer and more defined. The summoning is just as strong as it always was to reach out and help those who are seeking. It has a power all its own. A word here or there will touch this or that person, helping them to find their way, and in that I am honored to be a subtle part. The key here is that we never know which person and which words will have the greatest impact, so we must always listen well and speak with wisdom, not carelessness.

It is so important that we lead by example, not by force, regardless of whether or not we see anyone following. We are responsible for ourselves and our actions. If we mislead others, we are responsible for that as well. Integrity and impeccability are critical. I am honored to walk the path I walk, and I am humbled by the touching of lives. None of us is greater than the next. All are worthy of our love. Everyone will choose their path and walk it for their reasons. So the call to being a Medicine Woman or shaman is the certainty of living life in balance with one's own spiritual philosophy, in harmony with nature and in service to humanity and Spirit above all else. The call is indeed the journey of discovering how to live in this spiritual balance, but it is also the journey of the self, a journey that will be a great teacher.

The way you walk, handle challenges, face your obstacles, hold to your truths, place each footfall, each thought, and each word shows your integrity and your intent. It is the Will of Spirit that you answer to and the path continues until you get it right. There are times it may seem hard to find a resolution to your problems and make a clear decision on issues. If you take to Spirit only that which you cannot do yourself, you will find the choice makes itself. A personal philosophy consists of a strong will that says you must try by yourself first; it includes exhausting every known avenue to you, wielding the energy of the universe, and using all the tools at your disposal, be they mundane or spiritual. It includes making mistakes, learning from them, and moving on.

A rising consciousness is now taking place as a new heightened state of awareness. It is leading to altered states being experienced by many. For those individuals, life is seen as a spiritual realm that intermingles with the mundane world. It is the union of the two, where we walk with one foot in each, experiencing no separation. Acknowledging and paying homage through your own view of The Powers That Be, learning to honor these Powers as Great Mystery, is the key that will provide you with a union and philosophy that will encompass all of life. In learning to recognize the elemental spirits of the four quarters and the Guardians of Otherworlds, you will learn to honor the teachings of the world's wisdom. You will recognize the right of every individual to follow his or her own path wherever it may lead. By doing these things, a new and vibrant strength is revealed to you. Within its context is found the encouragement to seek spiritual development through freedom, growth, and enlightenment.

In the unfolding path of becoming a Medicine Woman, I came to realize that shamanism is not simply a cultural manifestation. As humans we all ask the same questions of who we are, where we are going, and what the journey will lead us to discover. We seek to understand the mysteries of life and death. The shaman knows the answers. The spirit deep within us is there to guide us along a natural path when we are able to recognize it. The Medicine Path is an enhancement to our lives. When we are conscious of our actions, and know they need to be considered for their consequences, and always seek to find greater spiritual growth and enlightenment, we are walking a Medicine Path. That walk is ever in the service of Spirit, Mother Earth, humanity, and All Our Relations.

I invite you to peruse the paths, the ways of a different perception of Spirit than perhaps you are accustomed to, and to meet your own conclusions. There are many bridges we cross in life. They come in many guises. Come, continue to take my arm and we may cross this one together. Learn what it is to be a peaceful spiritual warrior. Understand that for most of us the battle lies within as we struggle to find centering in harmony with life and balance within nature. Learn to mirror it with soul-shine. The magick is you.

Truths are not recognized as being "out there." We must learn to acknowledge them internally. It is my greatest hope that somewhere among these pages you will be inspired to see a truth that is yours, in that moment begin to seek its meaning, and express it upon a path of your own choosing. In this way you will come to understand the philosophy of your own spiritual path.

CHAPTER 3

DEFINING YOUR PATH

How we define our spiritual paths is up to us. Labels are forever being sought, but that terminology is simply a choice of words...yours. I offer the term "eclectic" throughout this book simply for its generic value, but it is your path, and you may call it whatever you want. You may be asking when you will be ready to create your own philosophy, and the answer is simple—when you have found your spirituality and realize you no longer need to ask the question. That same spirituality is different for each of us no matter what traditions we may have been fostered in or exposed to along the way. Our spiritual philosophies grow, mature, and Be Come what they will according to the paths we walk.

Be Coming a Medicine Woman is a process by which one attains enlightenment and lives life. It involves knowledge, practice, experience, patience, and training that form a state of being where the question, "Am I a shaman?" is not required, because the answer is known before it is asked. You study, you learn, you Be Come, and you are. You know when you are a "wannabe" who is only playing shamanism. There is no getting around Be Coming a true shaman, because a calling to the role is a summoning so strong that any resistance creates an internal struggle.

Aspects of the Shamanic Path

The shamanic path itself is an interesting one. It is a personal path to be sure, but it is also one in willing service to others. To serve all forms of life willingly from the very core of your being and live your life respectively is all that is asked of you. Through one's own perspective, an individual can practice shamanic ways without becoming a shaman. It is a versatile field of study and just as perplexing as anything else if you jump into it with both feet. When approached with discernment you will find areas that hold a strong personal appeal, guiding your path as it unfolds. The shamanic paths will lead to others, and a gradual evolution takes place. It is like anything else—it involves a good deal of work. The shaman strives to learn the mysteries behind the paths and grows gradually into wisdom. Through trance, meditation, visualization, and serious discipline, the areas of study become mastered.

Shapeshifting as Part of Your Path

An area of study that may be mastered over time is the art of shapeshifting, where the form of a plant, animal, or even a rock closely linked to the practitioner is experienced. A transformation takes place that can be either spiritual or physical. It requires great reserves of energy to undergo such a change allowing the shaman to travel into Otherworlds. Because the practitioners are using different life forms as vehicles for their own spirits to maneuver, there is obviously a great deal of training that must be accomplished to achieve success—dedication and impeccable intentions are required.

Some cultures see shapeshifting as spirit possession, while for others it is merely working with the power of an ally or Guide. In essence, it is for the purpose of soul retrieval, healing, enlightenment, study, or even to assist an individual in recovering one's own Medicine in some way. While it is frequently linked to the shamanic journey, it is akin to astral projection in many ways. When accomplished it can be a projection of the shaman's own inner spirit, or a shapechange into the spirit form of their totemic guide. The fundamental belief behind this practice is that any gain occurring in the material world must first take place in the spiritual realm so it may manifest itself physically. The links between mind, body, and spirit are not perceived as separate issues but as a whole.

Tools of the Path

All living things possess an energy of their own. This includes objects when handled in a sacred manner. They take on energy and become imbued with it, becoming powerful tools in the hands of a shaman. It is a residual energy, one that resides within the object. Thus the shaman's tools, staff, and instruments, even the sacred sites, become powerful containers that are to be cared for diligently. They are links to the realms of Spirit. This is why the energy is often very intense at a sacred site; it has built up from many years, usually generations, of specific use and intent. Other sites are built upon vortexes, where the natural lines (often called Ley Lines) of Earth energies cross one another, creating a whirlpool of spiraling vibratory power that can be tapped. The shaman knows these places and portals and uses them to further enhance their focus, Medicine, and workings, and through the use of sacred tools brings the two together.

The Portals

The shamanic path is one that endeavors to work in service to others, provides personal growth, involves meditation, trance, out-of-body experiences, and entry into Otherworlds through entries called portals. One such entry point into Otherworlds is a state of trance called the shamanic journey. It is a relatively safe and comfortable method for meeting and working with Spirit or one's Spirit Guides. It is a way of retaining your connection to the Seven Sacred Dimensions. These are deep connections, and the shaman walks between them all, serving where he or she is called. Centered, the person moves freely and works to heal, discover lost information, or become enlightened in some fashion. States of altered consciousness are achieved and various levels of trance are experienced.

Another portal of entry is found in the vision quest. This is a journey that is undergone by most individuals only once in their lives. The shaman experiences the vision quest as ongoing throughout the course of their Earth-walks. For the path-walkers, the quest will be undertaken repetitiously as it is assimilated, and transformations become evident.

Spirit Guides Along Our Paths

Many shamanic teachings take place in Otherworld settings. Because of this you will often find art in the forms of rock paintings (pictographs), carvings (petroglyphs), and land art (geoglyphs) at or near sacred site locations. These sites offer portals or entryways into Otherworlds. The art is highly symbolic, depicting events that can and will take place at a specific locale. By this, they become a shamanic record. Other Shamans would be able to read these symbols and work with them like a map. Many of these symbols are of a universal spiritual nature. They generally depict the Spirit of Place (local guardian spirit), or aspects of the shamanic journey through symbols. This is found throughout the world, and we have many such sites in America.

While the idea of having spiritual guidance along our paths is often difficult for many people to accept, Spirit does guide us when we are willing to learn the signs given as reference of what is about to happen. It is through the language of signs that I have learned to read life, to communicate with it, to know the nature of it. You can too. Gifts of power are received from Spirit and must be accepted along with the responsibility of service to others.

Accepting the Gifts of Our Paths

The ability to walk between the worlds is a gift available to anyone who wants it. It is the ability to see no lines of division but a unity instead. You will know how to recognize it when it happens because the worlds simply meld together. It does lend a different perspective on life. It is the melding of these worlds that allows you to focus at the snap of a finger, and you will always keep an ear and eye cocked. Your senses will pick up on things. When honed, they work like a tool to alert you to subtle shifts in the immediate environment or when involved in shamanic activity. This is true in the mundane sense as well as in a dimensional one. You will know when it is time to heed signs, such as shifting dimensions, messages from Spirit, Alerts, spirit presence, elemental presence in natural form, like wind or rain according to the given moment. Through the senses comes the ability to "read" or understand those sensations, trust them and act accordingly. Once you learn the technique of achieving this state of consciousness, it seeps within you and becomes a part of your nature. It is something you will recognize in a Medicine Woman, shaman, and the Elders: a calm, reassuring, peaceful presence that seems to reside in and emanate from them, almost as if they have an immense library of wisdom at their fingertips and know deep truths...and they do. This is why in Native American culture there is a great respect for the Elders of the Tribes—a respect we can all learn from.

In learning to read the signs, we must be patient. They will stir your senses and draw your attention. It becomes your focus ("trigger") and thus becomes a sign. Understanding the meanings of animals (their essence and nature) addresses the issues that present a topic of the message. The same thing is true of the elemental forces. If a sudden gust of wind stirs still air and rattles the leaves of a bush, you look at it. Your senses tell if there is intrusion, or help. The actual element addresses the situation. This is a sign.

It is not easy at first. Once the path is known, however, they are not so subtle. It is more like an alarm or attention-drawing magnet; something makes you do a double-take or focus away from what you are doing at the moment. Some people call this a sixth sense or intuition, but I believe it goes way beyond that. Having a sixth sense or intuitive moment comes in flashes; it is inconsistent. Walking as a Medicine Woman there is no flash, only the presence of the Now and the wisdom to recognize it. Signs may come that hold your attention for a time and then release you, like a touch from a hand that lingers hesitatingly a moment too long and is quickly withdrawn. These signs are what the centered individual is watching for, and their ability to meld between the dimensions allows that to be a constant in their life.

Connecting to Your Path

The Medicine Woman sees a link no matter where she is; whether alone in the countryside, or in the center of a huge metropolis, it really does not matter. The smallest things can say the most. A missed phone call or appointment, a message that alters a situation in your life, a sense received while shaking someone's hand, even eye contact from across the room that draws you away from what you are doing. It is something that speaks to you inside yourself to which you have learned to listen.

The animal spirits that come to us in nature, dreams, and visions tell us many things. The land's voice, that of the forests, and the voices of plants will speak to us of events taking place. The winds carry messages when we know how to listen. All these things speak volumes of information that most people ignore, yet they are the languages I have come to know as a Medicine Woman. Spirit moves in so many ways. All you have to do is ask for the guidance to recognize these things and then remain open to receiving them. Rest assured they will come, for there is no such thing as coincidence, only Spirit's way of getting your attention, holding it long enough so that It may impart a message and then releasing you to act on what you have received. What better way is there to find your truths?

Following and Growing with Your Path

Amid these skills there are hindrances as well, and we need to be aware of them. Quite often our emotions can blind us to what is taking place. We need to use them as triggers and then flip the proverbial switch to shut them down, taking the issues on with logic. Only then can we see clearly. Emotions can and do block our receptivity. Control is the issue as we learn to focus and achieve our skills after learning to keep ourselves centered and maintain the balance necessary to remain attuned to all of life. You will find that once this is accomplished, each day brings new issues to the forefront.

As you meet new people and begin to converse with them, you may be surprised to discover that you are expressing more and more experiences and enlightenments as if they were old hat. Just as often you will realize when you speak that you know the words are not your own...not totally. You will see them as inspired or find the words of others bring unexpected answers to questions or problems you have been seeking resolution for but not voiced. Moreover you will see the synchronicity of life that reaches beyond the boundaries of coincidence into the whole. The lines we draw define our realities and separate us from the center, and we cannot remain linked so long as we choose to continue to draw them. Call it a spiritual nudge if you will. As you delve deeper and follow your inner urgings to explore your path, the picture gets clearer and awareness increases.

Life is the greatest of journeys, and even though we think we know where we are headed, we are always being led to something greater by the needs of our inner spirit. Yes, you may accomplish your goals, but instead of the goal being the major issue you thought it was, in the end you find it has become merely a token. Other rewards are discovered along the way, and in reflection you will find them to be Gifts of Spirit that far exceeded your initial insights or anticipations.

Is it the Great Plan? Perhaps. It feels like it at times. You may have no intention of a specific journey bringing certain experiences your way. While there may be some anticipation of what to expect, each journey is unique. Each journey brings with it more than we can presume. At the level of the end result, we come away with greater understanding of what spirituality is all about and what shaman pertains to. This is due to inter-action with our guides and teachers of the spirit realms. They have the ability to see beyond our own scope of vision where our needs are con-cerned—and as to the actions we need to take to grow, for we are always in the process of a transformation. Our inner spirit does know and sees far more than we are able to. This allows it to gently steer us in the right directions, regardless of how difficult it may seem at the time.

The arrival is the end of a journey as well as a springboard to our next lesson. We are all born with a thirst that is never quite satisfied on its own. The inner spirit is the only part of us that knows the methods of quenching it, and we must allow that same inner spirit to quicken (stir with life) as it emerges into our consciousness. You do not have to try to keep up with anyone or anything. What is meant to come to you will, as long as you are striving to grow. Any opportunity to learn that presents itself and is not seized will come again in another form. Spirit in all Its wisdom will put it to you repeatedly until you understand that the oppor-tunities are endless. Certainly, the situations provide the lessons to come in different guises, words, teachers, phrases, ever-so-slights, but some-times that is all it takes to make the impression.

I had always heard that everything happens for a reason; now this is a common statement we all use quite freely. Like many other cliches, it is something I had come to take for granted. One day while I was in a serious family crisis a friend spoke those very words to me. Normally I would have smiled and brushed her words aside in nodding agreement, but she placed her hand gently on my arm and held my attention adding: "...and the rea-son is always good!"...in a whisper. I remembered the whisper. The lesson had come home like the snap of a rubber band. Now when things happen, crisis or not, I look for the good to come of it. It gave me strength, a subtle one, but a strength that I can pass on over time to others. It was a very powerful secret that she placed in my hands, and I know this was a good lesson, but there was another even greater: often the most potent mes-sages and lessons come as a small whisper...shhhhh...listen.

Finding Cultural Unity Along Our Paths

To some the shamanic path comes quite naturally through birth, and according to some cultures it requires specific training; however,

Spirit will teach anyone with true intentions to learn. I am attracted to Native American traditions. It is what I have had the most exposure to, and my friends have shared a poetic beauty with me as they taught me to see life through the eyes of their people. It just feels right. I know that many Native Americans feel the sacred teachings should remain cultural only. They feel that making them available to the general public is wrong. This has caused heated debates and more damage than constructive behavior would. I cannot help feeling in my heart that the Creator wants all those of us interested to be schooled in proper ceremony and spiritual guidance. The prophecy of the White Buffalo speaks of a time when shamanic teachings are to be put forth. The signs are here and the moment is now. Many of these signs are spoken of in prophecies. They are the events that foretell of a time of change. There were several relating to the White Buffalo Calf. These were met and signify that the time of the prophecy is at hand.

In fulfillment of the ancient prophecy, Miracle, the White Buffalo Calf, was born in Janesville, Wisconsin, on August 20, 1994. (The circumstances surrounding this event are discussed in more detail on page 54.) She is a shining example of the opportunity to share. And according to the legend, she stands for a time of peace and the coming together of the Rainbow People. She speaks of the need to share our wisdoms and take actions that secure the paths before us. It is a time of doing, and that doing includes teaching others. The very roads of the Medicine Wheel speak to the four races of humanity. Why so many are fighting against cultural unity but still claiming they want sisterhood and brotherhood is beyond me, except to say that their fears are making them selfish and allowing their shadow-selves to surface.

I must agree that the teachings need to be given accurately, that wisdom needs to be respected, and ceremony should be honored. I do not feel that one's race prevents any of that. As a Medicine Woman and minister I honor the teachings of all people while encouraging others to do the same. If we can learn from them and share in those teachings we only enhance our evolutionary growth. Yes, we honor traditional ceremonies and others that have been shown to us by Spirit. We do not close our eyes and ears to the world; we choose to open them.

While I cannot apologize for the mistreatments and wrongs done to Native Americans because I did not do them, I can feel that pain of injustice in my heart. I care about humanity, see the suffrages, the hate mongering, and can strive to do something better with my own actions. In my teaching, I strive to demonstrate by example how we as human beings can love, listen from our hearts, and hear the needs of All Our Relations. The first step in making this change comes with the acceptance of all life. We must try not to see others as different, because our needs are all the same. We are all brothers and sisters on this planet. Our spirits are of the same source, returning to it when we drop our robes. For these reasons I work to teach the wisdoms, and support the Rainbow People of the future.

In teaching, there is also an exchange where the student just as often teaches me. In this, continued growth comes to and from those of all ages and cultures. It is a way of giving and taking, for we are always in a constant flux of growth or adjustment. I have seen the face of Spirit in my vision quests, been touched by the Spirit of Place at sacred sites, and known the shamanic journey. If these things happened to me, a white woman, who came before Spirit with an open heart and willingness to be examined tip to toe no matter what, and if Spirit has accepted me as such, then why should I turn my back on my brothers and sisters? It does not make sense. No, I must pass the blessings on, helping all I can to find their way to their own truths. This is what Spirit has shown me.

I am not alone in this lesson, and there are many others who walk this same path. It is the attitudes of prejudicial minds that keep the world from changing, and we must work to make a difference. Once life and humanity are viewed from the heart, the lines of division vanish. We are a melding of our ancestors who mixed races more than seven generations ago. Today our families are not all pure-bloods, but we are pure-hearts. My own family has blood from each of the four races; we do not see lines but we do see love. No one can speak for tomorrow and say what will be beyond the glimpses Spirit grants us. Because of this, we can and should be mindful of the next seven generations. What are the things that will be left to them? The changes that need to be made come from a desire deep within our hearts first, then by allowing our eyes and ears to open and recognize what we are saying and doing. We are a part of the whole and together woven into the Web of Life.

It is such a blessing to grow with others who are willing to open their arms to those who seriously want a spiritual home and life that encompasses the teachings of Native American traditions. Simply creating such relationships has called for some tribal traditions to be broken. Sharing cultural teachings outside the tribal society is to break tradition. These ways, long held as sacred, are seen as the last vestige of a given cultural wisdom. Fear of corruption or of contamination due to sharing is common among native elders. To give them to the world at large is thus perceived by many to be a sacrilege, betrayal, and even a crime. However, these same relationships can be applied to and even honor the Medicine teachings, and the sharing that takes place.

In order to grow there must be change, or we stagnate. Tradition must change with the times or it ceases to serve its purpose. The teachings are for the people and if they do not receive them the purpose behind them is lost. By allowing others to learn, the wisdoms are preserved. Nothing happens without reason, and I do not see teaching the ways of the Medicine as a sacrilege. Certainly traditional ceremonies need to be guarded and honored, but sharing the wisdom is simply sustenance for the hungry. Gentle strength holds great power; it allows us to feel pride and respect for the paths that are walked in honor of the Creator in whatever form it takes.

We are living in a new time. I have seen the vision of the White Buffalo Calf prophecy, coming to know in my heart it is time for the Rainbow People to join together in peace, harmony, and respect for all of life. We have so much to offer and so much is lost by the lines of division. It is time for dissolving the jealousy and uncovering hidden truths permitting understanding to replace them. Respecting all paths and the sharing of good teachings to the dispirited of all races brings about a stronger unity. It supports and sustains us in ways that many who have lost their self-respect can come to regain it again. The only way people will learn to hear these truths is with their hearts. They must be given the opportunity to see how that is done.

Through those willing to set the example, guide and nurture, love and encourage, we make headway. We are never too old to learn the shamanic ways when our hearts and spirits are open to others. It takes courage to take a stand, to say you will walk the path of change. It takes wisdom to see when that time has come. The Medicine Path teaches us the way.

When we ride the wind, let the rains wash us, ignite the flame, look with eyes to see, and hear with ears that listen, then we come to know the heartbeat of Mother Earth as it is within us. By feeling the rhythm of our own hearts as the drum beats resound, by listening to the hooves as they fall and carry us into Otherworlds, we begin to journey. It is there that we go to find ourselves. We discover the residing inner spirit at our core. It is the life force that we inhale with our first breath and exhale with our last. In between these breaths is where we find our purpose in life, the reason we are here. We must find our ways to the center—the sacred space within and immediately surrounding our physical bodies—the center of the self and the energy it radiates. We must look through the eyes of our inner spirit, listen with our hearts, and see the world in which we dwell. It is there we come to see the Oneness that resides in All Our Relations.

Roles of the Shaman

A Medicine Woman is a practitioner recognized in a variety of roles. Each tribe recognizes the cultural, social, and spiritual role of the shaman or Medicine Person. This determines the variations in duties the role calls for in serving those respective needs and can be often influenced by the Medicine Person's abilities or gifts of power that can be applied to that service. Cultural recognition of a tribe to which the individual is affiliated (as a holy person, as a leader in the spiritual practices of the people) and circumstances determine how they will fulfill that role. Often these roles are separate positions within the cultural framework of any given society. Positions can be inherited by showing powers at an early age or being trained specifically by another shaman to follow this path. They can also be self-taught and learned from Spirit. There are those who gain their powers through ancestral heredity, often through gifts that may skip a generation. In any case, shamans will be initiated into the role they will fulfill in some fashion.

Individuals frequently show signs of being accomplished and possessing what can be termed as gifts, powers, Medicines, or magicks, which can come as the result of illnesses, accidents, visions, or other events that bring about near-death experiences and a sense of renewal or rebirth. Others walk the streets of the world unnoticed, living their lives as everyday citizens. All of them work in their own ways to be of service to others and honor their paths.

Sharing the Path

The shaman assists others in their initiations and vision quests. In this process the individuals are aided in the integration of their experiences as they progress along their path. Each individual will have his or her own unique Medicine or magick. Though others may share similar Medicines at times, there will always be slight variations. Everything has its own spirit and distinct Medicine, even down to the smallest grain of sand on an anthill. All are equal and none are more potent or valued than the rest. In some cases the Medicine Woman is a lore keeper, learning the stories that teach the Medicines received by others, and helping the student to understand them. Those focused in this area might be labeled a Medicine Chief. The stories draw pictures and in that provide answers, and if we are blessed with ears to hear they will enlighten us.

A friend of mine who has practiced Witchcraft for more than 30 years asked me to teach her about becoming a Medicine Woman. I laughed and told her she already knew most of it, but I would be happy to steer her in the right directions. At first she thought I was being far too simplistic with things, then there was a period of confusion during which she felt the teachings were too complex to fully grasp. I kept assuring her that we are the ones that complicate things and truths are very simple. As she began to sort things out, she realized that she is indeed an eclectic Medicine Woman and has a deep affinity with the path. Clarification came as she began reading and practicing what she gleaned from the teachings.

Today we share methods, and the wisdom of her prior path still serves her as well as it always has. My friend lost nothing in the process, but gained a whole lot more, and it was a pleasure to watch as she took yet another turn along her pathway of change. The role has now reversed, and it is she who is teaching me new enlightenments. Through her wisdoms I am gaining and growing in ways I never imagined I would go. Friendships do that. They inspire us to know, explore, and see what does or doesn't fit. Often we find we have been gifted with blessings to start the next portion of our journey.

Shamanism adds spiritual depths to the way things are perceived, going beyond mundane lipservice into a way of living. Shamanic practice is a matter of being focused and aware, seeing all the facets life has to offer, and being a conscious part of them as opposed to simply wielding or bespelling for selfish reasons. For the shaman Spirit is everywhere, and thus to connect to it is not a question of achieving, but simply being. By opening up and letting Spirit enter to touch the true self within us, we become centered. There is no true break in the path that lets you shift back to mundane life because you are centered in Spirit and always aware of the coexistence. There are triggers brought to our attention through the honed senses and the exploration of spiritual dimensions that help us to learn where to focus. As we grow in knowledge, we learn when these triggers have been set, and it is time to focus in one direction or another.

The Role of Shamans in the Community

While a tribal shaman will continue to fulfill the needs of his community according to custom, those customs have changed slightly over the years just as society has changed. Still, the role is there, and it is a position held in honor and function. When you think about it, the needs of individuals are basically the same. Our concerns are for food, clothing, shelter, health, love, work, dreams, goals, and our general environment. We all seek guidance as we deal with these very emotional issues, and many choose to seek answers through a spiritual path. The shamanic role within society today still serves the needs of the given community. It is no more specialized than that of a tribal setting, because there too is the individual's medicine (gifts or talents) as widely varied as the individuals themselves. Counseling, healing, readings, spiritual guidance: It is all there and then some.

If a community has a holy person or other ceremonial leader, the shaman would then work on other levels. If these roles are not filled, the shaman becomes the most likely candidate the community would look to in leading them. I know those who are solitary practitioners, others who are active in a community role, and still others who are combinations of minister, holy person, and shaman. Their roles all depend on the situation, and the needs that are to be met. We can be trained in many ways, but it is the synthesizing of that training that makes us what we are, determines our skill levels, and directs our paths so we may grow into who we are. There is a saying that variety is truly the spice of life, and among those of the Medicine Paths it is no different.

The Brujo

Shamanism has its dark side too. Among the Amerindian people there is a term known as the Brujo. This individual is a sorcerer who is greatly feared by the people. Self-indulging, often reckless in concern for the effects of their actions, and highly skilled in the arts of magick and sorcery, they are intimidating to most. While they can be good people, their role is seen in a negative context to the Medicine Paths. The Brujo does not serve the community as such, but moreover they are devious and uncaring as to the consequences others may suffer by their deeds. I guess you could say they are the bullies of the block, or the black sheep of the shamanic family. Very little is known about them and what is known is not freely discussed. Most people when asked about them will claim that such a person does not exist. A lack of discretion in this area can be dangerous, and many believe they would be cursed for speaking of the Brujo aloud. This is the negative side of shamanic Medicine as far as I am concerned and one that should be avoided at all costs.

Initiating Your Spirituality

The Medicine Path is one of many initiations, each taking the individual to yet another level of growth that is both expedient and phenomenal. I know this from firsthand experiences. As I underwent the initiations, I discovered myself evolving into a Medicine Woman, and the growth is continuing daily as my path winds its way through many new challenges. Because of this, and the needs I saw within myself, I realized that there are many others who were walking in very similar shoes and feeling there was much more that could be discovered if attention was just jiggled in a slightly different direction. I found this path to allow me to create what was right for me, and it can do the same for you. It will allow you to walk your path in a sacred manner all your own.

The Medicine Paths are just another form of shapeshifting into spiritual consciousness, and there is so much to be learned from the old ways. They will allow their truths to be incorporated into the new, and the eclectic approach will surface allowing you to adapt in whatever ways are required of you. Often these skills come in multiple forms that allow Spirit to be served in a variety of ways. That service cannot take place if we ignore our gifts. What we do with these Medicines and the way we walk our paths reflects who we are. It allows our paths to emerge and become our tradition. Yours is waiting.

CHAPTER 4

LORE AND MYTH

We learn about spirituality through experiences coming from associations within nature and dwelling within the shamanic reality itself. The lore and myths are intricately woven into shamanic practice and wielded as tools and classroom teachings for those who are seeking to grow. If you were to read a novel becoming lost in the story, you would have escaped, or journeyed. You can have the same experience when listening to myths and lore. They are such an intimate part of shamanic oral tradition and life that a union is formed. It is one in which the realities of life and myth meld together.

Instead of seeing the oral traditions as a collection of simple stories, the shaman lives and works with them, continually placing them at the core of those foundational studies. Therefore, in working with the myths, a transitional journey occurs where deep meaning is given to each telling and great power resides within them. For this reason, each telling becomes a classroom, allowing the shaman the opportunity to teach from the wisdoms they hold, and the listener to be swept away.

Striving to label all aspects and to revise these labels buries the myth in theory and that is not what I want to accomplish here. I want to bring you into the myth itself to demonstrate the shamanic perspective, for there is so much more to a myth than storytelling. This offers the best experience to shamanic truths that speak of heritage, culture, and spiritual beliefs. These tales become sacred and are given the space to come alive, passing them down through generations to those who find them new and exciting. Recognizing their truths as being innate within each of us allows the myths to tie our lives together. Through patterns that continue to emerge, we see them repeated in the generations that follow, and the spiral of life continues with each encounter.

The Value of Myth

Woven into the mythical lore are the Medicines. The myth is a spell in itself, holding us close to each event that unfolds as it demonstrates the exciting dramas that take form across our mind's eye. Through myth we gain enlightenment and understanding by recognizing and knowing well the characters who are in the stories. We hold the stories close to our hearts as we discover and rediscover their sacred meanings. We guard them, protect them, and keep them safe for future generations. We keep them in the forms of ritual reenactments and as songs to accompany the dancers. As sacred plays in ceremonies, they come alive each time they are presented to reinforce their spell.

The myth is meant to be fully experienced by all the senses and take us into an altered state of consciousness. When it is successful, it sweeps us away from the cares of daily life and into another realm. It paves the way for a mystical experience, for a shamanic journey, for a vision, for enlightenment, and for the truths to emerge and be seen once again. I am not going to argue or debate the validation for lore or myth. All too often they are given to being no better than wishes, ignorant explanations of nature, distorted facts, social strictures, cultural foundations, and any number of other precepts. The reality is that they are keepers of hidden mysteries. These secrets begin to emerge when the words are spoken. The myths may be different for each of us, but in a relative fashion they reveal the hidden ways and magicks of the ages.

Myths summon our inner spirits to acknowledge them and help us comprehend the mysteries upon a heroic quest or move us through tragedy, and lift us with the humor of the heart. Lore and myths are the stories and parables that are found in the teachings of all the world's religions, and their place upon the Medicine Path holds a powerful spiritual significance.

The Lines of Song

There are sacred processional roadways where myths are relived and songs are sung to tell of the lore and commune with the land itself. Altered states of consciousness are experienced along them as well as a deep sense of spiritual presence—they are "alive." These roadways are physically mapped out and followed with ritual acts rich in ancient tradition and ceremony. Some people are highly attuned to the land itself; they sing to it of how things were, how they are now, and how they may be changing. These singers know that the land is going to respond to them, that they are the shamans who are the caretakers of the Lines of Song, and survival depends on the songs being sung. The songs are alive and a way to give life back to the land itself as a form of sustenance.

The Song in Australia

Two hundred years ago in Australia there was one song sung. It was enough. It was a traditional song of the guardianship of the land. It tells of the responsibility and duty to love and care for it. It was sung to remind the people of how they were tied to the land and how they were its stewards. Today there is an imbalance due to ecological pollution and a departure from cultural caretaking of the land itself. The singers are healing the imbalances by addressing the damage and what needs to be done to correct it. The role of the singer is sacred. Their songs speak of the realities of the land along with what all its inhabitants are faced with. There is power in the songs due to the spiritual bond they have with the land and the energies they tap into when their songs are resonating.

This healing has given rise to a second song. They continue to sing the two songs, but now a friend of mine who is a shamaness and singer, is about to begin a third. This third song speaks of the new ways, the return to the land, the rebirth of Mother Earth, and of what will be. In time, there may even be a fourth song sung, and it is to be hoped that it is one that will sing the praises of a restoration and wholeness. A fourth song of a union of all the races and the completion of the great tapestry that is the woven threads of all paths. The power of the song is mighty. It is a way of preserving the lore, but more importantly, to the Australian shaman, the land itself is alive and intimately connected to the prosperity and survival of all forms of life. The land is what matters and the songs sung ensure its well-being. Just imagine the weaving that could come if we all took up our voices together.

The Song in America

This is the oral tradition and it still lives. Here in America similar acts have been carried out among Native Americans. Each tribe has its own variation, but the basic structures are the same. The Lines of Song become the sacred Spirit Paths. Some of these paths are still ritually swept, pilgrimages to sacred sites along them still take place, and rituals are still performed. Songs are sung, myths are told, dances are danced, and they are done with the same honor and respect as in other parts of the world.

Pilgrimages

The singers can be solitary, fulfilling a need the land itself has. More often, they lead the people on pilgrimages along the Lines of Song and sing to them of the myths that are reenacted. There are shrines along the way that serve as reminders of these acts and the scenes they are partaking of signal the changes in the myths. When they come to the end of their territory, the next tribe picks up where the border of two territories meets. As the people follow the shaman on their pilgrimages, a trance-like state takes over as they enter the proper frame of mind. When this happens at specific locations along the way, specific issues of the songs come to life. The myth is relived physically, mentally, and spiritually. It is a shamanic ritual that the people are allowed to partake of with a strong sense of community. The songs continue. The myths continue. The people continue to walk and be one with the land. This is how it used to be.

Rebirth

For a time the people fell away, and the old ways began to suffer, the land suffered, and it was not good. New shamans are coming forth today and there is a rebirth taking place within the second song. This one tells of how the land and people are today, how they have strayed from the first song, how things have been forgotten, and the truth of the pollution that exists. A proper song takes you into the Dreamtime. In this way, the myths are told and the unions between the land and the people are renewed in the retelling or singing. There is honor, knowledge, and spiritual experience that comes from the old songs.

The White Buffalo Calf

Come, enter the sacred space of the Medicine Woman, sit while the myth is told that takes you back to a place my friend, Advent, calls "Once upon a time when there was no time." Step back into the mists of the ages when the myths lived, and mysteries were known to be hidden in the lore of the people. Listen to the words as you journey, and enter into Otherworlds through what is spoken. Through the telling you will discover words that reveal many secrets that lay hidden in shadows only the Medicine can summon. Let the words trigger a new awareness that is ancient in its form, and aid you in bringing your inner spirit to the surface of your conscious mind. Look beyond the words to their meanings, let the pictures they paint emerge, understand the creation in its myriad of tellings. Feel the presence of Spirit within the balance of nature, and the forces of Light and Darkness as they battle for control. Let the words teach you of the wonders they hold; their enlightenment falling upon your own path and showing you your way as you search behind the Veil of Illusion.

Let the words show you those who walk in myth, the animal powers, the Gods and Goddesses, the Spirits of Place, the messengers of Spirit. Listen to the voices of the plants, rocks, the land, of the stars and moon and sun. Hear the secrets they reveal and let your senses come alive. Enter and explore their dimensions, know their wonders and their terrors and understand. Enter the world of the Medicine Woman and learn to see through the eyes of your inner spirit as you begin to walk among the Ancient Ones. Know they stand among us today, their voices still speak the truths and their words echo in our ears.

This Medicine Woman speaks to tell you of a myth that is living, of a prophecy that has begun to reveal itself. It is the lore of the White Buffalo Calf Woman. In Pipestone, Minnesota, there is a sacred site where the rocks are quarried by the tribes of scattered nations across the land. It was not always so. Many years ago the indigenous peoples of the area were at war. There was much bloodshed and the sacred buffalo was being slaughtered. Blood stained the ground bringing much pain to the heart of the Creator.

The First Encounter

It was during this time the White Buffalo Calf appeared to two men on the prairie. They knew it as a sign from Spirit and as the creature drew closer they watched as it transformed itself into the White Buffalo Calf Woman. One of them lusted after her and told his friend he would have her for himself. The other warned him not to, that she was sacred, but his companion would hear nothing of the wisdom in his friend's words. When they came upon her, the first man walked up to her and she knew what was in his thoughts. She told him he should do what he had in his mind to do. The second man stepped back as the first prepared to have his way with her. Just as he was about to take her, a cloud arose and when it had lifted, all that remained were the bones of the man. The second man stood in fear, but the woman's voice was gentle. She told him he had a true heart, that he would live, and should go to the people and tell them she was coming to bring them a powerful message. The man did as he was told and the people prepared for her arrival.

White Buffalo Calf Woman came unto them with a message of peace, speaking of many things and teaching them mysteries. White Buffalo Calf Woman spoke of the wars between the people and told them that the Creator wanted them to stop. She told them that as a reminder of the bloodshed, the ground there would always remain stained red, but that they might quarry the stone that is found nowhere else on Earth. They were told that it was to be used in the making of the bowl for the Sacred Pipe, which she presented to them filled with symbolism. The Spirit Woman spoke of how all tribes might gather to quarry the stone and meet, but that they would have to do so in peace only.

White Buffalo Calf Woman took the men aside and taught them their mysteries. Then she took the women aside to teach them their mysteries. Finally she took the children aside and taught them. When she was through she spoke to the people of a prophecy and time when the White Buffalo Calf would return. This birth would be marked by specific signs they should watch for and she spoke of them. The calf would be female, its sire would die shortly after the birth, and the calf would go through four color changes, one for each of the races of man. It would be a time that would mark changes in the world, peace among all the races, a coming together of all peoples, and a sharing of their ways.

When she had finished she left the camp and walked back the way she had come. The people watched her departure in amazement, seeing her shift form to become the White Buffalo Calf once again before vanishing into the distance. For generations this prophecy has been passed down orally to the people and they have watched for the signs.

The Birth of Miracle

The prophecy came to life on August 20, 1994, when a calf was born in Janesville, Wisconsin. As the prophecy stated, it was born a female and her sire died shortly afterward. She has passed through the four color stages. Her birth alone has been estimated at being one in 10 million, and the facts surrounding the prophecy make it astronomical. She is perceived as a miracle of faith. This perception is reflected in her name; she is called Miracle.

Visiting Miracle

People from around the world have come to see her. There have been ceremonies with blessings and many prayers offered by thousands of visitors. A symbol of unity, prosperity, and peace, this sacred creature marks a new beginning for humanity and the restoration of world harmony. She heralds a time of doing, of a second chance for all of us, of the future coming to pass. Her humble life has been transforming as representatives of dozens of Indian nations have come there to pay homage to her, as have others from all races and religions. Some pray, some leave gifts, some weep, and others feel a deep sense of peace.

Visiting Miracle was a very spiritual experience for me. I arrived and looked into her huge soft brown eyes to see the peace she bespoke of. I felt her peace seeping into me, and there was contentment that filled my spirit. A deep sense of harmony, of balance, of tolerance came over me, and I enjoyed her company for a time in silence. There was no need to ask questions of her spirit; it spoke freely to me and I understood. She is that gift of peace to the world. I thanked her for coming, left my offering on the fence, and knew her blessing. As I was ready to go, she gifted me with a tiny tuft of her fur no larger than my thumbnail, but it is a sacred treasure. I will never forget the feelings of love, understanding, and compassion that she shared. Her spirit spoke to me and I listened.

Many have offered to buy her but the people who tend this herd will have nothing of that. They have instead turned their home into a place where others may come and leave their offerings, say prayers, and give blessings, making it a very holy place for many. It is nothing fancy, a humble ranch inundated with visitors who are called to the side of Miracle...the prophecy that lives. She has returned with the gifts of White Buffalo Calf Woman once more. It is happening slowly, but she is renewing the faith of many in the process of uniting religions, cultures, and races, and she is doing it with her presence alone.

This humble creature is a modern example of the myth, of its presence and meaning, and in years to come she will slip back into myth as other generations tell of her birth, and as skeptics wonder. For now the time of change is at hand. From her teachings we have the knowledge that we are all bridges for others to enter into the new millennium. The cultural methods may vary, but the consciousness is evolving so that we may act to bring about the change. Miracle marks the beginning of a new age, of a world transition. What was once myth has become reality and will again slip back into myth. The cycle repeats.

Miracle's birth has brought hope back to the people. It has inspired thousands, and there are many who work to see the prophecy fulfilled. It is the time of the Rainbow People, where all cultures will meld. She is not the only prophecy of our times. These events are happening worldwide. There are visions and apparitions from all major religions showing themselves, and all the world is being shown an option for transformation. What will we choose? The White Buffalo Calf is a physical manifestation, her birth foretold generations ago. Within her resides the spirit of the White Buffalo Calf Woman, she who manifested directly from the White Buffalo to the Lakota People so very long ago. The last time she came she brought peace to the people; this time she comes to bring peace to the world.

The Myth of Great Spider

Some speak of the Earth and her energies in the myth of the Great Spider, whose web covers the world. It encompasses the Spirit Paths, the lines of energy and song that span the globe penetrating Mother Earth and reaching out into space. This myth conveys a message telling of a truth as if it were the truth. Great Spider began to weave her web, and as she did she wove the threads of life that were the lives of men. She gave a long life to some, and a short life to others. As she gave this life she linked each one to the next and in this way created the web that would sustain us. She taught magick to the people and gave them the alphabet so they could learn to speak and write. Bringing alive the lore and allowing the people to embrace the truth behind the story, the facts behind the oral teachings remain a constant factor, and this is why they are so highly valuable. They hold the answers to secrets, allowing the mystery to live.

This Medicine Woman will tell you that Great Spider is the symbol of eternity with her figure-eight body. She would tell you that her eight legs represent the four Elements and four winds, and that she teaches the mysteries of Spirit representing the Web of the World. She represents female energy, the infinite possibilities of creation, and the eight spokes of the Wheel of the Year (or turning of the seasons and cycle of nature) that is ever dancing. She teaches us the webs of illusion, the truth of changes, the power of attraction, and how to capture that which we desire. She can warn of entanglements as well as the value of writing our thoughts down and tracing our progress upon our paths. She shows opportunities from an objective standpoint, that which is beyond our immediate scope of vision, and encourages us to be expansive. She will attract our attention to things we have accomplished, and teach us to weave new goals.

This Medicine Woman would share the secret that Great Spider shows us—the need to honor male energy, the warrior side of our balanced natures. She would tell you often that Great Spider is seen to be reflecting the imbalances through our negative attitudes and breaking down of relationships, proving to us that ego is the illusion. She shows us that stagnation is only the failure to create, that resentment will destroy us, that we will become caught in the web of our own illusions if we do not heed her messages. When we celebrate the successes of others, when we celebrate life, that is when we begin to be creative ourselves. We grow more positive and our outlook expands. She will tell you to let her inspire you. Shhhh...listen to the voice of Spider, close your eyes and see.

Medicine of Myth

Whether or not you are Native American in genealogy, you are still capable of hearing the voice of Spirit in nature. These ways will speak if you will but learn to listen. Today you can choose to make a difference, to practice a mixture of many different teachings along your spiritual path. For those who make these choices, it will be found that they will serve well to create a wonderful fulfilling light that shines brightly for them to follow. We take the path that we harmonize with and work with that harmony; it is always spiritual, but we express it in different ways; we each learn our own song. Many of us are keepers of the myths, the lore, the stories, and in the sharing of them we help others to see. We create a bridge for them to cross over into the Otherworlds and help them find their own places among them.

Through the telling of myths, others will be touched. Once they are touched by the spirit that the spoken word contains, then they will act. As they are moved to these actions, the change begins. To hear a myth and be touched by it, the telling becomes etched upon our memories and we are able to share it with others who can benefit from it. The way you come to your path is of no matter. By this I mean you were called to it, and you answered the call in whatever way you could. Now that you are on your path, in the Now of the moment, that is what matters. The confirmations of signs come, and the voice that speaks to you will grow stronger. Many of us take our cues directly from Mother Earth, from the energies and entities of Spirit. We have learned to listen with a sharp ear and a soft one, to see through a sharp eye and a soft one, to walk with Spirit. In this way we walk the myths. We know a oneness has been restored as it should be.

In learning the mystery we are able to guide those who are seeking. The myths are our teachers. We go to them to find the answers that lead to other questions, and we leave these teachers for others that will help us along our way. It is a web of perceptions that we strive to follow and answers come only when we are open to receive. This is what the myth does; it helps us to open.

Truth Found in Myth

Some of us are not privileged to be taught at the feet of a shaman. This does not mean that we cannot learn. Spirit will see that we are self-taught if that is what we are seeking. It will show the answers to many of our questions that lie hidden in myths, legends, and folklore, for at their core is a sacred truth. Once these truths begin to emerge, we can see clearly the paths before us. You do not need to feel this is any less valid than any other teaching. How did the first shaman learn? How do the present shamans gain greater wisdom? Even if they are trained by another, the true lessons come in a method that is the same. These lessons come with the teachings of the lore, with the isolation of the vision quest, and with experience. If we are blessed to meet a teacher, then that teacher's stories may shorten our path, but only so that we may go at a faster pace to arrive at the next plateau. If we stay with this teacher and learn only what they know, we are handicapped. We are meant to follow the Spirit Paths, to move through the myths, to walk the worlds of dimension, to pass through the mundane and spiritual realities in union, to do, to act, and to accomplish. We are not meant to sit by the feet of another and remain there.

Let life bring you your teachers and meanwhile, keep your eyes and ears open so that you may learn the secrets and mysteries that linger in the shadows. We rest with our teachers, we rest with our myths, we learn our lessons, and then run off to wield the knowledge. We learn where our next questions will take us when we are granted enlightenment. It is a cycle that never stops. We must learn to be patient and kind with ourselves. That patience must be as enduring as Mother Earth has been with us. It must be as patient as Spirit is with our efforts, for Spirit is the weaver of the myths and thus the tapestry of life.

How the Myths Form Us and We Form Them

Learn to go at your own pace and accomplish what you are to do. If you rush through life, you gain nothing but a crash course. You need to savor it, savor the myths and see for yourself what lessons they hold. Once we listen, we will know our callings. The myths may be collections of words, but words have power. The words came from the thoughts in the soul of life, they surface in your mind to create visions, and to create thoughts, and thoughts are things. So you form your world from the wisdom of the myths. Through myth we become co-creators and give life to the old wisdoms. Through hearing them we take vision and in vision we give life.

The teachings of my path tell that there is first the Creator. From this source, from Spirit, comes the voices that speak its messages. These voices are the sources of the myths. The strongest voices will be found in Mother Earth, Father Sun, and Grandmother Moon. From them will arise the voices of the Elements, of Air, Fire, Water, and Earth, and from them come the smaller voices of the animal spirits. We must all learn the different voices to be whole, to hear the song and join in the chorus. The more voices you can attune to, the more the myths will come alive for you, the greater will be the message you receive, and the wider your horizon of perception.

We can all learn to be keepers of the myths and hold a good understanding of them so we can share in their teachings. Though the myths we gather may come from many cultures, we will find the similarities and the truths and become strengthened in them. I strongly believe that we are coming to a time where all traditions are being recognized as valid parts of a greater whole. I can see that through incorporating their wisdoms we can create a universal perception, or at the very least, tolerance and balance of understanding. The Web of Life is expanding. If you know a truth, express it to those who hear your voice, see your actions, and learn the tellings of your culture, then you share wisdom, which will allow them to gain understanding. Expressing truth through true emotion is clear to those who can receive it.

The myth is an emotional telling; it stirs the senses; it brings them to the surface. The Medicine Woman takes these thoughts and emotions, she understands them, sings them into being, chants them into visions, and speaks of them to those who need to hear. The secret is to listen to the thoughts first. From your basic truths come clarity. It is the clarity of the Medicine Woman's voice that speaks the truth. Thus we come to see in new ways. It is an equal exchange between the student and teacher, a fair trade act.

Heroic Inspirations in Myth

Myths contain legends of heroic deeds, of those who went before us to accomplish great feats of strength and endurance, of trials and testings that challenged the very soul. They inspire in us the courage to quest, to face our challenges and to succeed. They explain what cannot be explained in mundane words, and bring alive all that exists beyond the perceptions of mundane eyes. They contain the tales of creation, the prophecies of worlds seen and unseen. The personifications of Light and Darkness come together to teach the paths leading to enlightenment. The story itself holds the key to the lesson it gives and the application we can put to our lives. When it is seen from this perspective, it takes on a life apart from the story and the plot stays with us to let its truths come forth.

Myths contain the mysteries of life, and the oral traditions required that they be learned verbatim so that these mysteries could be preserved...like the words of a song. In the tellings they are then presented as they have always been intended, and the smallest of details are often as important as the largest of scenes. Ask yourself how many times in life you have experienced something that could not be explained by the mundane laws of this world? How often have you thought such experiences to be from the pages of myth and not reality? How many times have you heard the secrets that are kin to the old lore told only to have it raise the hairs on your arms or at the back of your neck, or to give rise to the kundalini of your spine? How often have your senses told you these were truths that could not be explained any other way except to say you "knew" them to be so?

Ask yourself how many times your logical mind has told you to keep silent or to deny the experience? It is the inner spirit that recognizes these things and brings them to your attention. It knows when the mysteries of the Powers That Be have been shown and it reaches out to touch your life in subtle sensations. Rising up to confront the logical mind and the mundane reality, that same inner spirit allows you to possess a more spiritual perspective. In this process your consciousness is heightened, but only if you open up and allow it. This is the mystery of the myth unfolding. The inner spirit knows that myths teach us value, integrity, morality, impeccability, as well as the cultural mores of our heritage. It knows when the myths take us into phenomenal times, lands, and scenes, where there is a truth that supersedes the phenomena and reaches out to touch something deep within us...something that says: "this is so."

By listening to your inner spirit and learning to hear its voice, you allow yourself the ability to spend time out of time with those of elder races, those of antiquity, and creatures that step from the pages of lost tales to know them personally. It will take you into Otherworlds, into Spirit, into realms that tax your mind and wet your appetite for more of the mysteries hidden within their wisdoms. It will guide you as you strive to place the pieces of your own puzzles together, as you seek the light that will open onto the path. It is the voice in the stillness of your mind and it will call to you in silent, haunting whispers: "return, come home, know the mystery, believe in the myth."

The Plight of Mother Earth in Myth

The patience of Mother Earth is residing. She is in pain. She has cried out worldwide, and her voice has been heard by many. Those who have heard her are striving to answer. The song has been raised again. Through the lands there are healing circles, gatherings, events where thousands are focusing on restoring, healing, and bringing forth spiritual enlightenment. People of all faiths are setting aside their differences to find their commonalties and embrace one and other. Cultural barriers are falling and when they do greater growth will manifest.

The patience of Mother Earth and the Creator is a show of the wisdom the ancestors told of in myth. The prophecies speak of it because there were those who could see that the land would need to be righted, that it would come at a time when the imbalance was strongest, and the risk to our very survival its greatest. They could see that the pendulum would need to swing back at a point or cease to swing at all. It is through the myths that these legends ring true to those who will listen. Each of us in our own way has a role, not forced by the minds of others, but inspired in ways we can best serve Spirit.

You might be on a path as a humble singer, drummer, dancer, myth keeper, healer, a bold and feisty activist, or any number of other journeys in life that would serve to restore the wholeness. Our own natures will direct us when we learn to make union with the energy of Spirit. This energy is not of the Earth alone, it is of the universe itself. The harmony of these sources allows it to flow and understand that the union goes beyond the myth to the Source. All life is sacred, all life contains this flow, and all myths hint at it.

There are many among the indigenous people that speak of the land and tell us that we cannot own it, that despite what a piece of paper may say, we are its caretakers. These are the myths of Mother Earth. They express how she provides for us, and in turn that we must provide for her. They tell us that the people cannot exist without her, nor she without them. Each supports the other. In that unity we become one with Spirit and the truth presents itself. Nowhere is this unity better exemplified than in what we have done to our Mother...and in what we are attempting to do to rectify it.

We need these myths, songs, dances, and lore. We need to honor and steward the land, we need to help Mother Earth in her restoration so that we can survive, so that all species can survive. Endangered species are returning to their numbers and some that were thought long extinct have been found to exist. These are the signs the shaman prays and watches for, the signs of hope and Spirit's answers to our efforts. It is in the corners of the myths that this hope is tucked, and it is passed on so that when its light does shine we can see it, recognize the truths, come to know All Our Relations abide in and out of myth. May it live in you.

CHAPTER 5

EARTH'S COSMIC FORCES

The universe is filled with many wondrous things that capture our minds and hearts. We are fascinated by the movements of the planets and mysteries of the stars. We are dazzled by the displays of the Aurora Borealis, in awe of the solar and lunar eclipses, and bespelled by the meteor showers that streak across the studded night. From the deepest reaches of space to the innermost core of the earth, these cosmic forces permeate every nook and cranny. This energy is also information that becomes an important part of a spiritual pathway. For many people it appears as a transparent river or currents criss-crossing the land. For some they are visible and for others they are merely sensed, but they can be tapped.

Historically, these energies have been recognized by spiritual leaders, and it is only recently that they have come to be known as Ley Lines. These lines, which take form as energy roads, often become physical roads as well, laid out to trace the flow of that energy. The term was coined by anthropologist Alfred Watkins of Europe in the 1920s. Today the concept has taken off into the New Age movement's teachings. Theories still abound, and there will be some variations depending on which authorities you research. While the knowledge of these lines of energy has a much older lineage, it is Watkins who has been credited for bringing them to our attention.

Spirit Roads

The energy lines tend to fall into different categories: Spirit Roads, Ceremonial Highways, Death Roads, and what are now commonly called Ley Lines. An overview of these classifications is helpful in determining the type of energies one is dealing with and how they can be used. Spirit Roads are visible to the eye either on the ground or through aerial views as physical roadways. Those that were used, and in some cases still are, represent the purposes of ritual and ceremony. The Anasazi culture of the American Southwest did not use them as territorial lines of division, but as roadways that served multiple purposes. Ritual pilgrimages up from South America and down from Canada utilized some of the roads, while others were there for the specific purpose of ceremony, such as initiations or other religious rites.

The infamous roadways of Chaco Canyon in New Mexico are known to be paths initially followed by the Anasazi and other tribal cultures that came after them. Many find it a mystery just how they knew when to make the pilgrimages and when the mass gatherings were to take place. A Medicine Woman would tell you that they knew when it was time to honor the turning of the yearly wheel by following the change of the seasons. The Anasazi created kivas, or wombs within Mother Earth, for ceremonial practices. The roadways lead to and from them, acting as ceremonial highways. There is a major dwelling at Chaco called Pueblo Bonito. It is a central hub where the roadways meet and it has a major kiva. It has doors that line up from one to the next, and it is believed by some that initiates would enter the chambers in a succession of ritual ascensions taking them in stages through Otherworld realms. Having been there myself, I have to admit that I can easily see how the concept holds validity.

The Spirit Roads are visible from the air and there are more than 400 miles of them mapped out in the Chaco area alone. They are reminiscent of the lines found along the South American mesas and Nazca Strip in Peru. The roadways, wherever they are found, vary in size and width. Some are narrow, measuring 15 feet wide, while others measure 100 feet or more. Their depth is due to use and manmade curbs of stone or earth. These roads stop and start for no apparent reason or continue on for great distances, which is common to the Leys of all categories. They tend to run straight across the land and through or over obstacles such as mountains, stone walls, trees, buildings, and in a course that is always obvious.

Spirit Roads fall under the classification of Ley Lines because of their ritual usages, and the energies that build up along them over time. Many of them actually follow the natural Leys and are purposely built on top of them. Like any sacred place that is well used, residual energy remains there and sentience can often be felt. These are consecrated grounds, and one might be considered to be trespassing on them if not a member of the local tribe, or at least if the intent for being there is not proper.

Walking along such a roadway with proper intent can cause dimensional shifts to take place. This can happen spontaneously to offer you a glimpse, like a thought or passing moment that is subtle and lasts for a moment or so, or it can be quite profound, lasting for several hours or more. A loss of time seems to take place while such encounters are experienced, and reality shifts in dramatically subtle ways. While we can only theorize about their shamanic uses in the past, Mother Earth seems to be hostess to some highly significant tattoos.

The kivas of Chaco Canyon are on line-of-site placements and connect points of great distance where signal fires were lit and watches kept. With their structures built partially below ground to simulate the womb of Mother Earth, they are round and had poles that were the size of trees reaching skyward and were topped with roofs. Often they contained a sipapu, which are locations in the earth where the Ancestors emerged onto the surface and life originated. Some sites are still actively used today.

Spirit Roads were considered those by which the Spirits traveled in and out of this world, and there is much speculation as to their overall purposes. I believe that many of them were also used as physical shamanic roadways with markers along them to indicate location for the shaman in flight. Such markers might be enormous geoglyphs or manmade aerial pictures of totem animals and other shamanic symbols. They may also well have been territorial markers to let another visiting shaman know when they had crossed certain boundaries. The combination of the two seems logical.

Ceremonial Highways

The next classification is that of the Ceremonial Highway. These are often known as a King's Road for the coronation processions of monarchs or religious leaders. They were lined by the people wishing to observe the processions, and they were maintained by the peasantry. They fell into the hands of religious leaders as time progressed, eventually even into the hands of the local governments. While the people may have long forgotten the sacredness of the roads, the wisdom of the original shamans would have secured their preservation. Such religious leaders were able to sense the energies and work with them, discovering the courses through which they ran. They would map them out and consecrate the ground they traversed.

Death Highways

Death Roads run in straight lines and are relative to the belief that the quickest way to get the deceased's spirit to the burial chamber, and sealed in, is of the greatest benefit to the living. In some countries these roads are also called Ghost Roads and are said to be haunted. There are the Ghost Roads of German lore that come to mind—haunted roadways steeped in colorful tales. There are others that purport such tales as well. The burial mounds of Europe (where roadways leading to them are often called Ghost Roads) are often stone structures or chambered barrows that are blocked at either end with upright slabs of rock or boulders. These blocks are suspected to be barriers to the departed preventing such wanderings while containing them in their earthly crypts. Similar mounds are found among Native American sites throughout the United States.

Over the generations, worldwide desecration and anthropological studies have disturbed these sacred grounds. Rumors of curses, superstitions, phenomena, and Otherworldly happenings surround them, adding to their myths. In Europe, those who chose to build their homes along these roads had to leave the doors open at either end so the spirits could travel freely, or they would risk the hauntings. This is often the premise behind a house being built over the road in an arched fashion so the inhabitants could guarantee an undisturbed life. Haunted or not, Death Roads have a link of their own to the Leys.

The Ley Lines and Sacred Sites

The Ley Lines that pertain to the shamanic experience are many. Spanning the globe in a web-like structure, they are enhanced by Mother Earth's own natural conductors: geomagnetic properties, natural radiations, electrochemical currents, the forces of nature, mineral veins and deposits, storms, fault lines, and volcanic activity. The list is a long one because all these factors and more influence the energies that flow along the lines. Vortexes, or nodes, are points of concentration forming the crossroads of power. These are powerful sites where many individuals of spiritual persuasion seek to heighten their own abilities by tapping into great energy reserves. The shamans of old sensed these locations using them as sacred sites, places for spiritual growth which lead people along the sacred way, and as portals to Otherworlds. They did not have the scientific data or maps to show them where to look but listened to their own intuition to guide them.

An excellent example of what the shamans of antiquity were able to accomplish is found at the Big Horn Medicine Wheel in Wyoming. Medicine Wheels normally have four spokes or paths that define the quarters each elemental force presides over. Here the Big Horn Medicine Wheel has 28 spokes, which is highly unusual. These spokes correlate directly to lines of energy that span the globe. Because each path represents an Element, direction, and spiritual aspect of focus, again the 28 spokes speak loudly but are not understood. This particular Medicine Wheel is laid out in stone and fenced in to prevent vandalism. While Medicine Wheels vary in size, depending on their purpose, so their pattern of use can vary. Some are highly ritualized for ceremonial groups; there are others that are small for personal use—a subject that will be covered later.

Some spokes follow energy lines that are said to reach as far away as Stonehenge, while others lead to mountain ranges in California or vanish in the hills and ridges in other areas. Big Horn appears to be a paradox of Native American culture and Otherworld secrets. Although it is a shamanic site built under shamanic direction, who it is that actually built it remains a mystery. It does not conform to any known indigenous practices, and no tribal culture today makes claim to it. Those that are in the area say that their legends tell of Big Horn being there long before they arrived. It is considered to be several thousand years old and another mystery.

Not all energy lines flow in a straight pattern, and many can be found following the lay of the land itself. Mountainous ridges, underground waterways, mineral deposits, as well as fault lines are all known courses they travel. A good example of these lines would be demonstrated in the Chinese art of Feng-Shui, a science of geomancy or divination of the earth's energies. There is a direct correlation to the yin and yang principles of positive and negative forces. The energy lines are not restricted by country or tradition.

Once discovered, whether it be by known sites or divination, certain things begin to happen and manifest for the individual that walks or works with them or their vortexes. Phenomenal events take place there and a study of signs, omens, or events that may follow afterward is often called for to get the full value of the experience.

While there are many known Leys, others can be found to exist through various means. Through geomancy, divination, dowsing, ESP, and for those who are sensitive enough, a recognition of the presence of either strong positive or negative energies along some land course is often evident. The vortexes themselves are locations where the power collects and whirlpools forces of upward or downward energy. This lends each site its own type of working, and an experienced practitioner will know instantly what to expect from a location after a short exploration.

The electric vortex will send energy outward and up, invigorating and charging the work and practitioner. The work done would be comparable to that of a Medicine Wheel in a clockwise direction for positive effects. The magnetic vortex will pull energy inward and down, drawing and charging the work and practitioner. The work done would be comparable again to the Wheel and run in a counterclockwise direction for banishing illness, negative habits, grounding excess negativity, or to release fears and negative baggage. The flow of power that can be used is present upon arrival, and tapping into it tends to activate the staid presence of that force to raise an even greater amount energy. It is for this reason that playing with them is not advised for the novice.

Channeling that energy has risks, and if you do not do it properly, there are repercussions. The electric node will serve your needs if you are seeking enlightenment and growth. If you are ill, depressed, or wish to enter the dreaming state, the magnetic node will aid you. Both types can be used for vision questing and it is not at all uncommon to find a Ley Line with a Medicine Wheel (often more than one) significantly placed along or beside it.

In many states there are known sites of burial mounds, and often there are crystals or rocks at these locations that hold great power and shamanic significance. Hot Springs National Park in Arkansas is a good example, with its healing waters and white quartz crystals, which are some of the finest the United States produces. There is also Spiro Mounds

State Park in Oklahoma, where Craig Mound is the most famous burial site. Here eerie lights in blue or yellowish hues are reported over the mound and surrounding area. It, too, is known for its quartz crystals.

Bear Butte in South Dakota has long been held sacred to the Sioux and Cheyenne Nations. The spirit of Bear represents the inner reflections, the emotions, and the insight a good leader needs to keep in balance. Here the legends speak of Bear fighting a monster, and when the battle was over, Bear collapsed, turning into the mountain. Many great leaders have and continue to quest at this site. Seeking visions and receiving their powers from Spirit, they return to serve their people. It is a place that lends itself to expansive thought, which brings out a natural desire to serve humanity while remaining humble.

Many vortexes are known to possess a Spirit of Place, spiritual guardians and teachers, for those who know how to approach them. Or they can be perceived as evil spirits by those who do not. Every experience is a bit different, and two people can easily go to the same site and have totally different reactions to it. A site may be visited several times by the same person who will have a unique encounter with each one.

The geomantic harmony of the land and its voice will often speak to you. Many such locations will be natural markers, sometimes manmade, to acknowledge spectacular shows at the moment of equinox or solstice. Imagine standing on a peak and shouting to hear your echo return from various points. These resounding echoes can be applied in much the same way as sonar and used in journeys, meditations, or healings.

The formations of the energy lines and vortexes also create what are called land temples. These are natural formations that take on sacred significance and have an innate harmonic center to them. In ages now lost to us, these were often the sites of sacred shrines, temples, or groves. Many of these places are so majestic that they call for nothing more. The Grand Canyon is a prime example and has many such locations within it. There are countless others in the world that lay nestled in canyons, mountain ranges, deserts, and remote geographic areas. Large in scale or small to the point of comfort for one individual, these locations have awesome power and can be used in very profound ways.

The Spirits of Place who reside in the vortexes are often keepers of wisdom, oracles, healing spirits, or teachers. Sometimes there is a combination of two or more. Faces often appear in rock formations, and it is said that they are the spirits of those who watch over the site. I have found this to be true. Sometimes they will materialize, but usually it is simply a presence that descends or rises from the ground with a definite personality. A sentience can clearly be felt by any who enter the area.

Heightened states of consciousness are the norm for such encounters, even if it is just the energy itself that is being felt. The perceptions experienced at such times are often life altering. Growth, transformation, and visions are also quite normal. If you do not know what you are doing, it may be that the site will leave you with only the "heebie jeebies" or creeps as some would say. Any shaman would tell you that it is the Spirit of Place sending a strong message to you to leave.

Phenomena

Phenomenal events repeatedly take place at different locations. Lightning storms are perhaps the most common. Ionization of caves will attract lightning, even when a storm is not present. For this reason it is important to know as much about a site as possible for safety. Different times of the day may be safer than others. This same ionization is conducive to altered states of consciousness and heightened perceptions. Dreams, visions, and messages are quite common. Some sites are more active at different times of the year (solstice or equinox) or seasonally. Others are more active and will wave or peak in hourly, lunar, or solar cycles. Some fluctuate randomly while others stay constant.

Many things come into play, and the study of animals will take you a long way in deciphering the formations in the land itself to indicate the nature of a site. Understanding shamanic symbols will help when visiting sacred sites with rock art. From them you will learn the animal spirits that inhabit the area, the type of work that has traditionally been done there, and what the site is conducive to producing. Symbols speak in a language of their own. The Flying Buck (airborne deer, antelope, gazelle) is symbolic of shamanic flight. Horses are the steeds that are ridden into the shamanic journey. Spirals, grids, and dots are all symbols of the veils to be parted between the worlds of dimension, some of which can be lifted at a given location. Different symbols are keys to unlock the doors that will open at that site. Some places have two separate groupings, one for the shamanic lore and one for the general environmental lore that may depict life there as well.

Hands are often the signs of healing, as are skeletons, skulls, or a skull and crossed bones. Ghostly figures may speak of death and rebirth or initiatory transformations that may or may not involve the Ancestors. There are advanced stages of trance experienced or undergone that bring about transition into higher levels of enlightenment. This often increases existing abilities or introduces new ones and changes the individual who is being initiated. A transformation becomes quite evident as a direct result. The list of transformations is a long one, but the symbols seem to be fairly consistent worldwide.

The Risks of Working with Cosmic Forces

Elemental Forces

The phenomena often lend themselves to the lores, myths, and superstitions that surround these locations. Ley Lines are embroiled in such stories from ages past, right up to today. Risks involved with the energy lines and vortex sites are not restricted to the elemental forces of nature, though it certainly includes them. It is believed by many (myself included) that the lightning strikes are actually a part of the energy charging process as it forces a surge and ripple effect. While this may be the case, it is also a very real danger for those who are working with Ley Lines and vortexes and are unaware that such things can occur. You can look at the Ley Lines as the nerves of Mother Earth, the electrical charges of lightning strikes as the recharging of her nervous system, and the sending of that circuitry as a communication process.

Elements themselves may seem spontaneously chaotic and strike fear in the hearts of those who are being disrespectful. Even ignorance can instigate such recourses. Sudden winds may come up with such force as to drive the unwanted intruder away. The same can be said of storms and driving rains that will pelt the intruder with rain or hail. The Spirit of Place may manifest and create a sense of terror. It may strike the individual in a physical sense causing an illness that can range from mild to severe or even fatal. Whatever the case may be, the individual is made to feel so uncomfortable that they simply cannot stay. They are urged to flee the location.

The Spirit of Place

Another risk is that of disturbing the Spirit of Place. It is a well-known fact that many sites are renowned for running off unwelcome guests.

One example of this would be the highway that is being built in Hawaii that has, for years, suffered the wrath of Pele, the Fire Goddess, for the disruption of her sacred grounds. Workers have been injured and killed, machinery has ceased to function without reason, and whole sections of the roadway have collapsed despite the expertise of the engineers. Who is to say she is not present and exacting her due? The Spirit of Place may call upon the Thunder Beings and the Fire Sticks may be thrown at an individual.

Anytime you are faced with a new Spirit of Place, there is a challenge put forth to you to stand up to it or flee. If you stand, you must open up to the spirit willingly and let it examine you from head to toe. The willingness to expose yourself and be confronted by one's own shadow nature tells them your sincerity, and it shows your intent. Shadow nature is the dark side of ourselves. It contains bad habits or traits we would often rather deny than face. It is the side of our persona we tend to struggle with to achieve self-control. Your willingness to yield this part of yourself to be further purified, accepted, and given up in a sacrificial exchange for what you are about to receive is what the spirits are looking to see. They are also expecting you to challenge them. To stand your ground is one thing, but you should also ask who they are, what they want from you, and what they intend to present to you. Ask always if they are serving Spirit. Demand the same things from the spirits that you must give of yourself. Ask them to tell you their names if they will, and know that they will expect you to introduce yourself. Do not order these spirits around. Introduce yourself respectfully, demonstrating the honor you hold for the path you walk and all that Spirit brings to you.

It is important when at these locations, you remain centered, face the challenges head on, and stand your ground. You may feel an acceptance once the challenge has passed, and an embrace by the Spirit of Place is not uncommon. If you are not intending to work there, feel you have intruded, or received a warning, by all means leave. I have not had such an encounter and have only heard the tales from others who did. Once you start asking questions you will find there are usually plenty of people who are willing to share their story. You can check with the local historians to find out many of the local legends. I have been made welcome at every site I have gone to, and I truly believe that it was because I went in reverence and with impeccable intentions.

When a site is approached with honor, when you have cleansed and purified yourself, and you enter with the proper intent, you will find you are welcomed with open arms and gifted with amazing experiences that range from subtle to intense. You could be gently told to go, that it is not a place for you to work. To be asked to leave a site that is not conducive to anyone other than the attending shaman is not a shameful thing. It should simply be honored and another site sought. Such messages often come as a gut feeling, discomfort, and recognition that it is simply sacred ground through an inner knowing. To ignore something along these lines is just plain foolish. Even when our intentions are of the highest order, we can still be asked to leave. At the same time, sites can call to us, summoning us to their gifts and enlightenment.

The pendulum can swing wide in both directions, and I am not trying to discourage your use of these sacred sites, but I am trying to convey where the lore, superstitions, or myths find their basis in truths, and how to deal with it if you are confronted. Certainly any grounds that are on Native American property or actively in use by tribal people should be respected as such. Permission should be gained from the tribal leaders first.

Work Slowly and Cautiously

It is important to ground yourself after working with the energy lines or vortexes. I would caution individuals wanting to work with such a site to confine their work to one site per day, or walking one Ley Line at a time. Going from site to site can not only create an overexposure, but it can create mixed receptions from the variety of energies. This works against the body's natural energy flows. Headaches, nausea, nervousness, and other symptoms may arise. The overexposure can result in a residue of foreign energy in your system. You might feel buoyancy, giddiness, extreme exhaustion, confusion, vision problems, or some similar effects. Most of these are short lived, but there is no sense in pushing the issue if you do not have to do so.

Any sense of physical imbalance that leads to successive illnesses should be grounded. Caution and practicality are of importance. Learn to attune to your own body and inner voice, then to the site to find the balance, and be able to see the warning signs when they start to arise. Some people experience euphoric states, levitation, and out-of-body experiences, as well as dream states that are vibrantly unique. Journey work, vision quests, and meditations are all enhanced by these energies.

Many sites are conducive to physical, emotional, or spiritual healings, or any combination thereof. There are even psychotherapists that work with groups, taking them to these locations for just these reasons. Such work often involves strong emotions and can reduce an individual to tears. The experience can occur from the simple, overwhelming joy of encountering these positive energies that are present. Sites for healing have been known to help individuals through blockages, which are issues that prevent the individual from progress toward enlightenment in their spiritual growth process. These include, but are not limited to, their innermost fears, suffrage of pain too severe to face, cultural or religious beliefs or taboos, family traditions, and social values. For people confronting their innermost fears, it can be a very traumatic experience.

Spiritual Self Discovery Through the Cosmic Forces

Pay attention to your dreams after walking a Ley Line or visiting a node, as they will often be very significant for several days, perhaps even weeks. I cannot stress enough the need for journal work following a site experience and the nights of dreaming that often trail behind it.

Perhaps you will be shown a new animal or spirit guide at a site or in a dream, and the lesson will continue to follow in successive nights as you learn to work with it. I have gone to a site where seemingly nothing happened only to discover later, through dreams, that I was being contacted in that fashion. One just never knows for sure what the results will be, and they can be just as productive this way as any other. Sometimes a lesson will be imparted to your subconscious while you are there. These manifestations can occur in the Dream Lodge, and it is there that we can be given clues to many marvelous teachings.

Working these dreams out can take anywhere from days to years. What we perceive from Spirit may be comprehended, but expressing our understanding is very difficult because our perception is far beyond words. Whatever messages come to you from such experiences need to be heeded so that personal symbols can be understood. A key to understanding these symbols is the first thing that comes to mind when you see them. They trigger an intuitive response in the individual. When the same response takes place repeatedly with a given symbol, it takes on deep meaning that is very personal. Do not be surprised if the dreams themselves repeat to bring home the lesson you need to grasp.

People often encounter their Guardian Spirit, Totem, Power Animal, or other teachers at these locations. The work is intense when it comes through like that. Shapeshifting can and does often take place. Imprinting, where the spirit throws itself into your body and merges or passes through you, also occurs. Do not be surprised if you go to such a place and find flashing lights of neon or phosphorescent intensity. You might see balls of colored light that seem to dance in the air and have sentience to them, or hear sounds from stone mountains. Voices, apparitions, faces in the rocks that move and shift or seem to speak to you are all just as possible. These are parts of the myths and lore that surround such locations and experiences. I have known many of them.

Leaving a Sacred Site

It is important to leave the site as you found it. Often shamans will leave their token gifts or materials there in the rocks and crevices for return trips. Please respect these objects and the ribbon ties or tobacco ties you may find. Do not disturb them. If you arrive at a site and there are others ahead of you, wait your turn politely. It may be a long wait, but you would want the same consideration. If you cannot wait, go another time or seek a different location. If you decide to stay, be certain you let others' energies subside before you approach. Ritually cleanse the area first before beginning your own work. One just never knows what rite was done prior to arrival.

My warnings throughout this chapter have not been to frighten you. They are to impart the need to be serious about your work, honor the land and spirits that dwell in it, and respect the energy lines that web our world. Know that the Ley Lines run above, on, and below ground, penetrating the depths of Mother Earth, and out beyond the farthest reaches of our universe. It is a fascinating study, and once you become involved with Ley Lines, you may easily become attracted to working with them. Once you channel this energy, you will know what it is to tap Source Energy and Earth's Cosmic Energy; then your work will be highly improved.

You may begin to see the Ley Lines and nodes if you have been unable to before this. The flow is like a translucent or transparent river, or a light dusting of snow falling through the air with silver or multicolored lights instead of flakes, or wavering objects that range from shadows to brightly colored hues. We all see and feel things in our own way. These forces are the foundation of the Medicine we wield, and it is through them that we can tap into the richness of our cosmic heritage. Once you have been exposed to them, you will see why spiritual leaders the world over have placed such great value on the knowledge of their existence and gone to great lengths to protect it.

The New Awareness

Outsiders come and seek to own the land. Governments take it over or society encroaches, while civilization spreads and builds upon it. When conscious awareness of what is truly sacred takes its rightful place among us once again, it will be a change for the better. This new sense of heightened awareness that is coming about today—the return of so many to the shamanic and pagan pathways, the struggle to correct the imbalances of nature and the land—all this is pointing a strong finger, indicating the directions from which our future is coming at us. It is a part of the Native American prophecy and lore.

Our consciousness is raised so we may act consciously to bring about the change. It is a part of the nature of things. I believe that the land will speak to those who will listen. Each of us in our own way has our role to play by letting our own natures direct us as we join the union of the land and the energy of the Ley Lines and Spirit. We all take the path that we harmonize with and work with that harmony to find our ways, learning our songs and dances with life. Our exchange is to understand one another and thus better understand ourselves.

Cultural barriers are falling and when they do, greater growth can take place. It is good, and the Ley Lines are a part of it. They carry energy. That energy is information and information brings enlightenment. So through the tapping of the Web of Life we can all find union, coming to know the sacredness of Spirit in our lives according to our own paths. The patience of Mother Earth is a show of her wisdom. If we are patient, working steadily to progress in an orderly manner, and if we come together of our own free will, that same patience will be rewarded with advancement in path-work and personal spiritual growth. This is not unique to any one land, for all lands are timeless, and each of us is a part of it. We are not in any way divided from anyone else.

Through tapping the energy lines, we learn and grow to become spiritually wise. The secret is to listen to the thoughts first when singing the Lines of Song, or working with the Ley Lines. Your own clarity will stem from the core of their truths. The Ley Lines are energy roads, the paths between the worlds of the mundane and Spirit, and upon them are found portals to Otherworlds. In working with them, you will discover that even though the teachings of a culture are not granted to you in a tradi-tional sense, they can be found mingled upon the energy lines. It is not a line of delineation or one that may not be crossed, but one that tells you to turn now upon your path and seek another direction that will hold a more powerful way of teaching you.

You will learn to go with the flow of your life, and not to fight it. Ride your own nature as a bird does the wind. How will you walk your path? Will you notice that people of the world and migratory animals sense and follow these energy lines in their movements? Will you be aware that life teaches the lessons, Spirit teaches the soul, and there are many tools placed along your way? There are those we meet who can teach us their wisdoms for a time, those who will walk our path with us now and then, and then there is the Spirit of Place that resides where they cross.

You are your journey, and the only boundaries between you and the rest of the world exist because you put them there. Understanding this will allow you to travel, to access whatever is needed by tapping the lines of Earth's cosmic energy. The shaman uses the drum to focus. It becomes the hooves of the steed that will drown out the material world. Then, slipping the veil, it allows that journey to follow these mystical roadways. So it is that the land has come to speak to us once more if we will listen, if we are willing to touch the energies that travel through its surface and body. If we will honor it and respect our place upon it, then we will have made a change we can take pride in as a contribution along the way. We will have restored a piece of the myth, strengthening the use of the Ley Lines (which will truly become Lines of Song once again) and become more aware of our relationship to all of life. This is the way the Medicine Woman's eyes see the world.

CHAPTER 6

SEEKING BALANCE

In the process of finding balance when we are enthused by our spiritual questing, we can often lose sight of our priorities. We may discover that we have been setting our family, friends, and mundane affairs on a side burner. This can lead to all sorts of upsets and confusion requiring an adjustment or we will very likely feel as if the stars are screaming at us. Striving toward higher thoughts and ideals can come to a screeching halt when we find they are not present when we want them to be. When individuals seek to validate their views and cannot do so, it stops them from progressing. This will continue until they are able to work at discovering the area of concern. They must name and confront that blockage. This can cause deep pain in our lives, and sorting out all the perspectives is not always easy.

The pain we feel can be our greatest teacher as we explore the shadows and fears within ourselves. It is often like this during growth, both at the onset of the path and as we make our way along it. No one is proud of all they have done, thought, or experienced. In looking at our lives, we have to banish the negatives, and cleanse our spirits so we are worthy of the growth we seek. That cleansing draws on emotions and passions, meaning we must search our souls to set them right. We all would like to paint rosy pictures of our lives, letting the shadows lie in darkness, but until we can confront them we are only fooling ourselves. We have to be willing to open to Spirit and say: "Take me as I am, wash me clean, and teach me."

The Walls We Build

Most of us start out in youth unafraid and accepting as we begin to experience the reality of life. While it can be wonderful and bring about enlightenment, it can also cause old painful wounds to resurface as we move forward. When we are hurt there is a natural tendency to vow we will never let ourselves feel the pain again. We build barriers to the emotions and fears as we erect walls around us. These walls are strong and they work. As time passes, we tend to forget our wounds, letting them sink deeper into our persona where they become lost in darkness. Taking the walls down again means confronting our pain and digging through our emotional dirt to find why they are there in the first place. That is very frightening, and we often fight very hard to avoid enduring these inner confrontations.

In reliving old wounds, we are brought to harsh realities as we cry out or shudder. Facing them means we have to find new thoughts that will allow us to grow. The rewards are there at the end of it all, but until then it can be a highly intimidating experience. The most dreadful things can, in the end, purge us if we embrace them, love them for what they taught us, and then release them from their prisons. As we must tear down our walls we set ourselves free. The deconstruction is rewarding when it is done properly, and it is the most liberating feeling to own the freedom that it brings.

The Role of Acceptance in Creating Balance

If we start to draw lines on spirituality for anyone, we harm ourselves as well. What works for an individual is what works, and if they are eclectic in nature, finding things here or there that can support them in their search, then I applaud them. I see nothing wrong with discussing or sharing spiritual views and wisdom. We all tend to want to share our experiences and if others can gain from them, then there is value in that exchange. Sharing techniques and borrowing from one another promotes growth. Letting others decide what is right for us leads to frustration. The only way to true happiness is by listening to your heart and following its lead.

If we were not meant to follow our paths, Spirit would not have seen fit to send us teachings in the first place. Each person must search on her own if her path is to have meaning. We are all looking for a way to touch the face of Spirit, know the energy of life, and work with it productively. There is nothing wrong with sharing heritage, tradition, or eclectic wisdom. By exemplifying our beliefs, there is a sense of freedom that is invigorating. We must each judge what is right, wrong, true, or false for us to follow our own paths and find personal truths.

Finding Balance Through Native Spirituality

There is a beauty and poetry to the Medicine Woman's ways that stirs my spirit far more than any other path I have come to know. When it touched me so deeply in the beginning, I had questions of my own because of the cultural lines. My friends who were Native American quickly pointed out to me that "All Our Relations" does not simply apply to a culture, it applies to all those who live upon the earth. To my mind this made a lot of sense. I found I was able to tolerate others better, understand their needs, and know mine were much the same. This brought me into a harmony with all faiths, allowing a sense of balance to emerge. I continued on that path and I have never regretted it.

Frank Fools Crow was a Medicine Man and Ceremonial Chief of the Teton Sioux. He promoted multicultural sharing and teaching in spite of the fact that many of his people held views against that idea. He met with leaders of countries to promote spiritual expression and the tearing down of lines of division among the races of the world.

According to Fools Crow, all people are welcome to learn the Native American ways. He worked for peace among all people without judging by their race or cultural background. He was more impressed by the way they followed their paths. There was resistance from his own people for his beliefs, but it did not stop him from following his vision. To his dying day, he promoted healing between the races and the paths that would lead others to Spirit while serving his people, his community, and retaining the honor of leading the Sun Dances as Ceremonial Chief of the Teton Sioux.

Spirit has taught me over the years that as long as my intentions are proper, the technique I choose to work with is acceptable. I learned that if I need trappings (tools, regalia, and accessories used in ritual ceremony), they are there for me, not for Spirit. To honor Spirit is enough. So regardless of the academic views others may hold, I think the highest authority I need to continue along my pathway is that of Spirit and no other. The original spiritual leaders learned directly from Spirit and shared their wisdoms with their people, teaching us it is quite natural to turn to Spirit and ask for the truths to show.

We can indeed look to our own heritage and culture first, but when that does not hold the answers we are seeking, why should we stop? There was nothing in my ancestry that called to me the way the Medicine Path did. It was there I heard the subtle voice of Spirit, so for me it was right. If you learn to look and listen, a pathway that stands out will appear, feel like home, and be right for you. Taking a stand is a choice only you can make. Becoming comfortable with your own spirituality, something many seek their entire lives to accomplish, allows you to walk without fault and follow a path that is fulfilling.

Discovering Your Spirituality

Spirituality is such a personal issue that no one can dictate what is right or wrong for someone else. If the words of another contribute to our own enlightenment, if they make us think about our paths and actions, then they are blessings. Even in arguments there is wisdom to be shared and gleaned. Perhaps the words are more important than even the individual that authors them realizes, especially when they produce a positive effect. By lending grace and dignity to small matters, we can then give deep, careful thought to those of greater consequence. In this way each sequential stage illuminates our lives.

There is no quick fix to developing spirituality. Time, effort, and patience bring the rewards as we gradually Be Come who we already are. Certainly there must be a readiness on your part, a willingness and openness to accept the teachings you seek from whatever source is available at a given moment. The teacher takes many forms, and may come as a thought, a voice on the wind, a quotation in the morning paper, a line on TV, the words of the child next door, or from an old sage on a park bench. The teacher is everywhere, and it is up to you to extract the wisdom by asking the right questions.

A good teacher will guide you in finding your answers, not give them on a platter. You just do not learn the value of them that way. That is why some say "reality strikes." A truth is known the moment it is presented because it is a truth and therefore cannot be denied. That is the irony in life. Just as a spiritually developed path exudes grace from the inner being of those who walk it, there is little need for superficial personas. We can hope for things, but we get what we need more so than what we want— and in the end value it most.

I have always felt that it is the purpose of the individual to find spirituality on his or her own terms. Unless it comes in that fashion, it is meaningless. To discover your inner spirit, set it free to guide you, and reaching your spiritual goals and potential is the true meaning of life's quest. To love, learn, and perhaps hold a little wisdom in the process helps to gently maintain the balance. The irony in Spirit is that it simply exists and to find it we need only go within ourselves, looking into the smoking mirror that reflects who and what we truthfully are.

We can clearly, and sometimes painfully, examine our own nature to discover what is important for us to grow. To understand a lesson's truth we must accept the teaching, for there is no amount of effort that will make us learn it unless we are open to receive it. The Dream Lodge is a place of being in the Now of the moment, where the dream within you rises to the surface and your inner spirit awakens. It is the place where the dreamer becomes the dream and your Guides can speak to you freely of many things, of mysteries, for all answers lie within.

When transformation is at hand, a turning point signals the change to come. A stillness takes place, bringing about an inactive time when you can do little else but reflect on what has been and what you are striving to achieve. There is seemingly no headway then, for the movement is within you to guarantee eventual success. A time comes when we turn from the dark shadows within us back into the light of recognition, and know what we must do. It starts with the stillness and moves to the quickening, which is the manifestation of a motion towards a birth. The sensing of a life force—like the first movement of a fetus before it takes place. Then the birth of transformation begins.

Stepping Onto Your Path

It is very common to sense an eagerness, a need to push ahead and try with all our might to make things happen. Unfortunately, it just does not work that way and one cannot push the future. These times require us to allow our feelings, impressions, and desires to seep into our spirit so that we can later bring them to the surface with conviction. We cannot move into the fast lane and expect to be complete, because too much would be missed along the way.

The new momentum brings about a recharging of energy, and we can then sense when the time is right to go deeper on the spiritual path. At times our inner spirits demand rest and will not let us expend our energy too soon. They know there is a need to renew, recuperate, trust, and carefully develop our spiritual lives. We are repeatedly taught that true healing and progress stem from the balancing of body, mind, and spirit. It seems simple enough and in truth it is...once you attain the ability to differentiate between them.

The body is of the physical realm, the home of our five senses. The mind is of the mental realm where logic and reason are the processes that bring about the actions we take. Spirit is the life force within us that links us to Great Mystery, permeating all that exists as well as our own inner spirit and higher consciousness. Learning to balance the three becomes simplified once we understand this and the manner in which each functions.

Understanding can enhance our paths and bring about a sense of well-being as enormous transformations change our lives forever. This balance, when achieved properly, opens the doors to limitless possibilities. All it takes is the will to bring it about, and it is our spirit that acts as our inner guide to accomplish just that. By shifting our perception, a trigger is released that will shift our realities; that shift brings new light and clarity and is the basis for many teachings. We learn that all energy is intelligence and we can virtually breathe in our enlightenment.

The Mirror of Shamanism

Shamanism mirrors the inner spirit, allowing the individual to recognize a connection to the Creator and acknowledge his or her own abilities. The inner spirit is attracted to nature, recognizing that the doors to Otherworlds of reality are hidden there. In nature we are lulled into silence, a silence that makes room for the voice of that spirit to be heard. The whole of its wisdom is grasped the moment its voice comes through to the conscious mind. Truths are instantly recognized and life becomes a pursuit of that wisdom on a conscious level. That is the moment when we begin to see into the Otherworlds and realize that they are a part of our own. We are of Spirit, the source of life, the embodiment of all that is, was, and will be through the exchange of pure energy. It is ours to tap.

We need to learn not to argue with our minds, but to still them so we may see the truth. Floating inward we can let our breath carry us. We begin to sink deeper until we are engulfed by our own spirit and able to see through its eyes, to perceive through its wisdom. Floating, sinking, arising, we come to the enlightenment. If we are lucky we will get a glimpse of things through the eyes of Spirit. It is done without expectation, and we must allow the stilling of the mind to make way for what the spirit within will reveal. The trouble is that most of us are born with minds that are easily distracted, often confused, and uncivilized when it comes to working with our inner spirits...we are raw.

Your inner spirit is the part of you that witnesses the physical and spiritual worlds. It tries at times to reach out to you to indicate important issues or warn you of danger. Initially, it does this by stirring your senses and emotions. Its voice grows stronger through the use of your intuitive powers, and greater still through meditation where you will actually learn to hear it speak to you. To listen to this voice is to be conscious of your spiritual link to the universe, its cosmic forces, and Spirit. Your spirit will know when the connection is made. You will have an innate understanding of all that occurs in your life. It will come in a flow of information that does not need words to express itself. Learning to perceive the physical and spiritual worlds as interconnected parts of the whole, as the macrocosm of the outer universe and the microcosm of the inner universe, is a major breakthrough for the modern Western mind. Most people do not have the dedication it takes to remain focused, but once achieved it brings about a deep awareness. Like the roots of an ancient tree that reach deep under the earth, with its limbs reaching up into the sky, we become centered amid the dimensional realms; our energy is like the branches stretching in all directions. Centered, we become the shamanic tree. The shaman knows this tree well, and it is one of life's greatest lessons.

My telling you these things is not enough. They must be experienced. By taking time to examine them closely, understand what we represent, and know what we are willing to give up to comprehend the mysteries, we are able to grow. The price is not any higher than you are willing to pay, but it is just. Only through self-sacrifice, by yielding up parts of ourselves that are no longer supportive to the ways we are growing, can we gain headway. This can include bad habits, old views, ways of behavior towards others; releasing the negatives brings a transformation by creating a space for it. Spirit then moves through us to fill that space, making us better aspects of ourselves and humanity.

Most people react with the modern Western mind seeing the reflection of the physical body. A few may realize that we are but a breeze that has passed through the worlds of time and dimension. In truth we are all of this and more. Within each of us is found the four basic Elements of life: Air, Fire, Water, and Earth; the same Elements that are linking us to Spirit by asking us to examine their traits within ourselves. This includes questioning who we are, our purpose in life, and reflecting on the answers within us. The shamanic path is one of self-discovery and spiritual evolution.

Who are you? Better yet, what are you when you look at your reflection? These questions are the constitution of the Medicine Woman. They are the teachings that allow individuals to have the unique ability to look beyond an act to see its end result and know if the act is worth doing. Those who walk the Medicine Path do not waste time and energy on useless pursuits, so each act becomes one of carefully thought-out purpose.

Rebirth of Spirit

We are all creatures of habit, and we need to learn to break the old negative patterns in order to disown them. The shaman experiences death to learn it is but another phase of life. It is an end to an old cycle and the beginning of a new one in which rebirth follows, and there is no need to fear. This is often a symbolic death and is frequently a major portion of stages of initiation that must be undergone so the person can be reborn. The shamanic death can be physical in the case of near-death experiences through illness or unexpected events. It is returning to life with a new outlook or change in personality because of that experience. In either case, the fear of death can no longer exist because one has experienced it and has the answer.

Exercise: To Go Within

Walk with me into a brief exercise. Taking my arm, breath in and out slowly. Feel the inhalations and exhalations as a continuous swing of the same pendulum. Let yourself sway with the rhythm. Life is death and death is life. It is all one. Feel the shift of your awareness from time to timeless, and understand that consciousness survives death, be it physical or spiritual. Step between the worlds; let your body float on the sea of breath.

With each inhale and exhale you will ride a wave that carries you into the next realm. Reality simply exists wherever you are. Recognize this experience, the natural laws that are governing it, and its presence.

Breathe in and out, and feel the passion of adventure surge in your veins. Recognize the consistency and feel the solidity of this moment. Know the reality of your inner spirit tends to be intangible and does not lend itself to a tangible examination, but will yield to the reality of the Now. The spirit that dwells within each of us exists within your body and outside within the dimensions of Otherworlds. Let it rise up to the surface and settle itself back again. Know the illusion of the physical world and that it must be recognized in order to be overcome. Linger there and let your senses reach out and touch the energy around you. Take time to feel it. When you are ready, follow your breath back to the surface.

You have just passed through on a brief journey. It did not involve a lot of time, but your body should feel quite rested and your senses alert. Having been gone only a few moments, you experienced what is known as a dimensional shift. Look at what you have come to know for yourself in this short process. Did time have relevance for you? No. In other dimensions time is not the factor that it is in the mundane world. Learn how to step in and out of it and back again feeling refreshed. It has only been a small step this time, but it is a beginning and you will come to know greater ones. You may want to make a few attempts if your logical mind is stubborn, but with practice you will come to see what I demonstrated here.

The Inner Spirit's Quest

This is the quest of the spirit as it strives to take you deeper into the dimensional realms and make you more aware of wondrous things. It strives to heighten your senses, your consciousness, and to let you see. Once you have this initial phase mastered, you can then open your eyes when you arrive, but not your physical eyes. Open your spiritual eyes to experience landscapes and places that are to say the least awesome. You can expedite this through longer periods of meditation, creative visualization, dreams, and ultimately through vision quests. There is no way to understand it other than through the experience of it. You can grasp the theory, but that is all you will have until you accomplish it for yourself.

In the stillness of a moment of silence, in the space between the heartbeats, you become one spirit melding into the unity of Spirit. This union allows you to tap the cosmic consciousness and to enter into enlightenment where all answers reside. It allows you to take things a step farther and rise up with your inner spirit from your physical body to project into the shamanic journey. It allows you to comprehend the vastness of the love that Spirit embraces all of us with...a love that embraces all of life.

This same love will wash away negativity, sorrow, pain, and set you free. Its invisible permeation is so complete, so magnetic, that it effortlessly draws to it all other forces adding to its power. It dissolves anger, fear, illness, and any other negative force that comes into contact with it. Sorrow cannot exist where laughter dwells, and you will feel like laughing. Therefore, arm yourself with the swords of love and laughter, see the humor in the simple truths. Wield them unconditionally knowing that as you treat yourself, you will also treat the world. If you are unselfishly giving acceptance from within, you become your sword and it becomes you. An inner spirit that has been cleansed properly and becomes balanced does not seek to possess, dominate, or control. It seeks to abide within its center. It is free to reject negative traits as needless, transforming them into positive aspects of pure love within the heart of the spirit. No one needs to fear life. Simply seeing each day as a new beginning, a chance to start over or continue on your path; seeing yesterday as a lesson learned; and seeing tomorrow as a great possibility allows you to live life to the fullest. By accepting what comes and facing it accordingly, you will come to see that positive and negative conditions are two coins in the same purse. Spend them or save them...the choice is yours.

Positive Affirmations of Balanced Spirituality

If you are confused, you can pray and request an answer, and if you remain open to reception it will come. Affirm your goal daily and send this message aloud into the realms of Spirit. Show your intent. Live it. Be it. It is in the realm of Spirit where it will be heard and acted upon first. Simply requesting what you want, accepting it will be so, and then releasing it is enough to give it birth. The clearer your intent, the better your results. The simpler your request, the stronger the flow of energy that comes from it. That is why many ask for the "right" situation, circumstances, or occurrences to take place, leaving the details to Spirit.

In this way you will come to see that as you receive, so you must give. Your gift then becomes a part of you and you give it to the world from the endless well that you drink from. There is no need for selfishness, though it does creep up on us all from time to time to test our character. When this happens, all we need to do is say aloud: "I feel selfish and no longer wish to do so." Breathe in and out, taking in the feeling, embracing it, loving it, then exhaling to expel and release it. Repeat the process until the feeling is gone. Expel all images and emotions connected to it. The universe will embrace them and transform them into positive energies that can be used elsewhere.

Transformation takes place and becomes more profound the deeper you look within yourself. Examine the essence of who you are, the person you wish to be, and the love you feel. Look into the light of your own spirit and the shadows as well. Find the things you must rid yourself of and release them. This may sound easy, but it is often very painful and takes a determined will. Let the light of your spirit shine forth. Become your awareness of pure love, proceed to walk your path, and create a spirituality that is right for you.

Walking your path in this manner allows you to manifest who you truly are. That heightens the chance of surprise encounters with spirit or phenomena. You may experience premonitions, a strengthening of your will, a focus of your intentions, or some positive form of growth. It attunes your senses to recognize the opportunity to expand your knowledge. Once you make the connection, these happenings grow in number and in strength as you develop your skills. They are the things that make others think you are psychic and have abilities beyond the normal range. The truth is that we all have these abilities to varying degrees, and you are simply learning to exercise your spiritual muscles and wield them.

The exhaled breath of negativity and its counterpart, the inhaled breath of purification, will take you into the fragile realm of your spirit and act as a trigger to your logical mind. Awareness of breath then becomes a link for you to put one foot in each world and walk in unity between the two, dwelling in the Now of the moment. The Medicine Woman knows that time disappears when focus is placed on the Now. In the Now you dwell in union to honor that part of you in all that exists, and in that act you will honor Spirit. Spirit will begin communicating with you on an even stronger level once this transition takes place.

Recognizing the Hand of Spirit

When accidents happen, you will know Spirit is seeking your attention to say you are out of balance. When they are avoided, you are listening and centered. Stay alert; the signs will be there for you to read because

Spirit is always speaking. You cannot do this if you go blindly through the material world denying that Otherworlds exist. When unusual events take place your quickening has begun. Ignore the events and you are back to square one. Work with it and you will grow in understanding.

Life is a treasure hunt you must ever be questing to resolve. Its treasure is the wisdom you gain and the love you earn by giving that love back to others. Once this is realized and accepted, the path you follow becomes automatic; it appears beneath your footfalls. That which is given to you to desire is from Spirit; aim for it, but do not struggle, as Spirit will bring it to you when the time is right. You will recognize it when it comes. Life is a gift, and to desire what it offers is your right. It is a right that you should not judge, but seek as a process of growth. Part of that growth is making room for it by discarding old desires you once had. You cannot fill a glass that is already full.

Shout into the wind and your voice will be silenced. Play with fire and you will be burned. Stand in the rain and you will get wet. Kick the ground and you will stub your toe. Yet, by going with the flow of the wind your feet will be fleet and your voice stronger. Use fire with respect and you will have light and warmth. Wash in the water and you will be cleansed; drink of it and you will quench your thirst. Lie upon the ground and you will have a bed; walk upon it and you will have a road. Know then the spirit of matter and walk between the worlds.

Spiritual Ethics

Spiritual ethics are the ways a given individual guides their walk along a Medicine Path. Beyond them lie the many traditions formed and unformed that you may choose to be a part of, and the many realms of dimension that you may choose to enter. The basic fundamentals of all spiritual paths remain consistent within cultural variations that can be followed, but the rest is up to you. You might ask: "But what of spiritual ethics?" They exist as well. What would be your spiritual guidelines? What would be your book of rules? You should follow your own sense of integrity, and your own rules by which you guide yourself. These must ever be questioned and examined. You must know what you stand for, and then strive to exemplify it. The ethical values you place upon your pathway, and thus yourself, are an expression of its validity. They serve to distinguish your path from the paths of all others.

There is a strong union found in those who walk the Medicine Paths. In the simple sharing that goes on between the many diverse communities, a strength is offered to all of us. Resources are available today that far exceed those of only a few years ago. This is especially true now that we have the Internet, which allows us to reach all corners of the globe. Those of the shamanic paths are tempered in their spirituality and have much to offer. There are many in the mundane world that are coming to this realization. Those who are tempered become the steel that forms the bridge others need to cross over to reach enlightenment.

It is our obligation to the many who are confused to eliminate the distance that confusion creates. This is not an issue of force or a crusade, but one of friendship and benevolent sharing when our paths cross. I have been active in that role for many years and find that as we draw nearer to the new transformation upon the world, more people are asking questions and seeking answers. The distances are growing shorter.

We are drawing closer to a universal understanding of what spirituality truthfully means. This is bringing to the surface tolerance and compassion for all paths. I do not see this as any form of being restrained in expression or modification, but an enhancement to humanity. It is a tolerance for race, sex, and religious or spiritual paths. In doing this we will come to see that the ties that bind can set us free when we give them wings. I hope to be a simple feather in that flight.

Power does not reside for long in incapable hands, and the Creator will test everyone. To walk without intent and integrity is to fool the self, and the fool inevitably ends up with the wrong end of the staff pointed at him. To tap the true energies one must know how, and the greater forces do not respond well to those who demand. Experience teaches this to everyone. I do not believe that the gifts of Spirit come to those who do not deserve them, nor do I believe that they can be wielded with success by incompetence. A student of theory only is half blind and will remain an apprentice.

Sharing wisdom is a question of respect, and I respect all choices of paths that people make when they follow their own inner voice. More than that, I respect and honor Spirit. I have been gifted with the love and leadership of many teachers, honored to learn a variety of tribal teachings, and I have been blessed. If things are meant to be known to us, Spirit will find a way to get the messages out.

Shamanism versus the Shaman

The majority of people tend to follow a shamanic tradition of some sort, which is much different from being a shaman. The shamanic tradition is more about the spirituality and personal relationship with Spirit than it is to claim any title or powers. In that process, as you develop your relationship, Spirit often bestows Medicines or gifts upon you, and in that process you Be Come enlightened and hopefully much wiser. Titles are for others to label you with and some are to show respect or honor, but when you know yourself, that is enough. Just as the presence of Spirit permeates all of life, constantly shifting and changing form to be all forms, our paths permeate life and become all things to us. To have the right relationship with that blessed presence is not wrong.

It is time to dance, to honor the Rainbow People, and for those of conscience to come forth. Listen to the voice of Spirit before you listen to the voice of hatred or prejudice. Truth is where you find it, and to seek balance as you create your own path will bring joy into your heart. It will make you come alive...perhaps for the first time in a very long time.

CHAPTER 7

FINDING SPIRIT

The union of reaching out and touching Spirit brings about a mystical transformation. It touches your soul as it confirms the experience. Knowing about the interconnections that exist in nature brings fantastic enlightenment, deep fulfillment, and an abiding sense of peace. To witness the mystery of the energies reaches beyond faith to a knowledge of outgrowing social tunnel vision. Narrow-mindedness simply cannot exist in a moment like that. We are all searching for our place out of time, our sanctuary, where we cannot be found unless we choose to be. It is where we reside deep within ourselves. It is the true Now, the timeless center, the door that opens to us when we know how to knock upon it.

The subtle ways of Spirit call for us to remain open, but we can be blinded by our attitudes and must choose to see. We learn to wield our natural tools that become a portal to other realms, teachers, and greatest of all to Spirit. To accept the call of the vision quest is to spend time with Spirit and be granted a vision that will guide us through life. To pray and be heard we must cry our words, feel them in our hearts, and then be still so the answers may come. To feel the energy of Spirit and different life-forms, discover what you are connected to, and to accept kinship with all of life without an intermediary is to know a profound truth. Yet that experience alone is only a hint of what can be tapped or discovered among the spiritual realms. The experience brings firsthand knowledge that is in itself a tangible thing. The essence remains with us always.

Most answers come directly from awareness of the Creator, as you discover you can center yourself by going within to the spirit that resides in you and knowing that it is a connection to the intelligence of the universe. To know truth resides is a powerful path to Spirit. It feels natural, calls to you, draws you in making sense at a root level. The beauty, love, and peace that comes with the closeness to Spirit manifests when you open to it. In getting to know Spirit intimately, there are many different methods available. As you explore them you will find yourself developing a unique style of presence in the process. You must meditate, pray, and give yourself permission to seek enlightenment, to seek spiritual growth to experience validation of the dimensional realms willingly, and quest for an encounter to take place. Spirit will respond, establishing a firm relationship and understanding of the path you will follow. This comes from the undeniable awareness of a new reality.

Finding Spirit in Nature

There are many who say they cannot hear the wind speak; they do not know how to listen. It is done with the soft ears of your inner spirit, hearing with your heart and senses, not the mundane ears of the physical body. Once you learn to do this, the physical ears become attuned to the spiritual ones and the voices the Medicine Woman knows will guide you to Spirit. You become sensitive to cues and know when something is telling you to take heed. It is done with the soft eyes of your inner spirit, seeing with your higher abilities and becoming attuned to them. The physical eyes then join that attunement and the sight that the Medicine Woman knows will reveal Spirit to you.

Moving through the elements and nature, we come to see that life exists beyond its physical presence—everything has a voice. Trees communicate with us. They speak at a slower rate that makes sense when you think of the speed at which their sap flows or the pace their roots and branches take in growth. They are slow-moving entities; we call them the Standing People, and they are very wise. Because they are stationary, they are observers and will teach you how to observe as well. Try standing in one place facing only one direction and just looking at everything you can see within your scope of vision. Do not turn your head. Just look at what you can see with your eyes. At first it is a scene, but as you become like the tree, you begin to see the finer details. You notice the movement of plants and animals and the elemental forces as they all mingle to create a symphony and dance of life. Think as the tree would think, slow, methodical, and patiently in an enduring observation.

Watch. What is revealed to you will step beyond what you first glanced. Already you have learned a new way of seeing life. One way you can personally connect to trees is through their leaves. Link to the leaf energy, go between the leaves to the shadows that take you into Otherworld settings. Trees have a very lulling sound when the wind passes through their leaves and their branches begin to sway. It is very easy to let that lulling sway cradle you, then slip into a semi-trance state of deep meditation. Sitting with your spine against a tree, or using a root for a pillow while lying on the ground and looking up into the canopy, even hugging the tree, makes you aware as you come to feel the love it exudes. You can work with different trees exploring their various natures. You can work with woodlands and forests as a single entity with one or many voices.

The relationship between you and the trees is based on your personal desires and needs. Find a way that makes you feel comfortable and become one with the tree, woodland, or forest. Feel its essence, and open to its wisdom. As you do, a sense of the life force in nature becomes crystal clear, and you start to feel the presence of Spirit as it permeates all that exists. Suddenly you realize that Spirit truly is everywhere, and you can join with it at any time. You can become the Air, Fire, Water, or Earth, stepping beyond their physical presence and entering into their spiritual nature. This allows you to see their sentience, to feel it and know they are alive. Gradually these unions expand your awareness and you begin to focus on the whole of their dimensions. At that point the face of Spirit becomes clear; you unite with it. It is sort of a melding together as you come to understand that you can communicate. You need to get out there and experiment with various techniques to find what works for you.

The little "trick" of listening to the tree is the same "trick" to hearing the Voice of the Land, Wind, plants, elements, Standing People, Stone People, Animal Spirits, or Spirit itself. All have a presence within them, all are alive, and you are eternally linked to one another. By going into your core and attuning to your own spirit you learn to touch the center where the life force resides. It is from this center that sight, hearing, touching, feeling, and tasting become heightened, and you sense life as the Medicine Woman knows it. At that point you can open yourself to the softer side of spirituality and step into the Oneness. Open yourself as if you were shedding a coat or swinging open a door to greet a precious friend.

There is total trust at this point. You need not seek that out, for it resides in the knowledge that what you are experiencing is a reality. That trust allows you to accept the truths as they are presented to you and know the Oneness of Spirit. You can extend your thoughts and begin to open a channel of communication that is amazing. Tears of joy may be streaming down your cheeks as the reality sets in, but you will be laughing at the same time to know how simple it all is.

Finding Sight

Sometimes to find the "sight" we have to soften our gazes, looking at the world through slitted eyes and letting the mundane world slip out of focus. The Otherworlds will begin to open as the Veil of Illusion slips away. The weight of the physical world falls to the wayside and you suddenly understand the terms of density and vibratory frequencies, not in scientific terms, but in those of spiritual perception. Use them as labels if you need to; I tend to feel my way through them and work intuitively at this point rather than on an intellectual level. It is simply going with the flow of energy. Sometimes the currents are faster, sometimes they are quite agitated, and at others they are like a slow lazy river. As you feel the currents, you come to see that is the "pace" set in that dimension and you can match your own rhythm to it.

Spirit then comes into view through a myriad of manifestations. Once we realize that we are our own gatekeepers, we really see the need to keep gathering our keys. Each person born is gifted with her own way of touching Spirit, each is given signs to read as he walks through life, and those signs help us make our choices to wield these gifts or to ignore them. Perhaps it will be a sign that tells us we are to wait for a time to wield them, or a nudge to begin exploring a specific gift. When the call comes it continues to sound until a conscious decision is made to either move ahead or stay where we are.

The Call to Spirit

The call comes in many forms, and often in signs that repeat themselves throughout life. Suddenly we realize that we are in communication with Spirit, and if we choose to we can walk a path of enlightenment and heightened awareness at all times. We can know the Medicine. It is the integrity with which we make these choices that allows for our spiritual evolution. The guidance must come from an attunement with our inner spirit so that we know what is right or wrong from the core of our being. We have to trust that same inner spirit, knowing it is the true self within and that we are not separate entities. We have to realize that we are spirits with bodies, not bodies with spirits. That makes all the difference.

Deciding to reach out, coming face to face with Spirit, is a major step and a leap of faith the first time. Once this is done, a new insight allows the enlightenment to touch you, and in that the knowing that you can return to this place of abiding with Spirit any time you wish. After that reality is realized, you will know what to say when you are asked: "How do you know what you are doing is right?" or when you ask yourself: "How do I express this to others?" The answers will come, your inner spirit will guide you then, and you will simply know when it is right to do or say things in your communications with others. Before any of this can happen, you must learn to listen, and that comes through meditation, prayer, and vision questing; it comes through dreams and time spent focused on nature and the basic elements.

Attuning to Spirit

Spirit is always present, and attunement brings a feeling of being watched or accompanied by an unseen presence. You will get a sensation within your body—hairs may stand up, a feeling may quiver in your stomach, or other senses will heighten. It is a knowing that you are not alone that is pervasive within the environment. Sometimes you will be challenged and must stand firm, secure in knowing you are seeking a truth and deserve an answer. You can feel the power in the air and simply know when you have been accepted. Spirit will guide you from that point on, showing you things in ways that will leave you awed. The subtle moves made by Spirit become bold when you open to them, and all it takes is the right frame of mind.

There may be a struggle to ask the right questions at first. Sometimes it is best just to experience the shared Oneness, finding comfort with that. In this way you can take what you need from the moment and answers will seem to surface within you. It is a telepathic communication, though you may speak aloud if you so choose. The comprehension is so pervasive that you will know when you have been gifted with enlightenment by feeling and seeing through this new perspective. The truth is undeniable, and you will be given choices to stop, continue, or return another time for more.

Sometimes Spirit will teach you a chant, song, or dance to be done when your gifts are to be used or when you want to summon the essence of other entities. It is amazing and moves you deeply when this happens. When I saw the power of my song for the first time, I wept as a feeling of deep respect and awe filled me. I knew it was something that could not be taken lightly and was a very important tool to possess. Whatever transpires in the union with Spirit, it is followed by a period of assimilation and a seeping-in of what took place. A time of absorbing all that Spirit has revealed to you and what you are to do with it is necessary to assimilate how you have been changed, challenged, and accepted.

Sometimes you are asked to sacrifice in order to receive. In a fair exchange, that is well worth the price you are asked to pay. Sometimes that sacrifice is demanded of you and at other times you can determine it yourself. If you do not know what it is you need to give up, Spirit will make it abundantly clear. The process repeats itself as you grow over time, always cycling and ever spiraling higher. If you are looking for deep spiritual truths, they can only prove themselves through your own explorations. When you have met Spirit face to face, when you have had communion with nature, when you have worked personally with the elementals and their forces, you come to see that the great illusion is the physical realm in which we dwell. There is indeed more than meets the physical eye, and the lifting of the Veil of Illusion reveals this.

If you took all the people in a given room, each one would have his own perceptions. If this same group of people had experiences in which they understood the illusion, you would find that through those experiences there would be a general consensus, an understanding of what took place. You would also find a variety of explanations as to how that happened. There is a timelessness to spiritual truths and that certain something that continues to call to us, that speaks to the very depths of our beings. It strikes at us with its sincerity and honesty while the realization becomes immutable and universal. This constant searching for the truth is a part of each and every one of us. When we search hard for things they elude us. It is in the gentle probe that they reveal themselves. When we relax and go with the flow of nature, of ourselves, when we open wide to receive, that is when Spirit enters, permeates, and exits to display the answers to all our questions.

To witness the face of Spirit leaves us feeling awestruck. This is the intangibility of the tangible...a paradox of dimensions, of what is, is not, and still is. Truth rests in the eye of the beholder because we each perceive it through experiences that validate it for us. The shamanic path teaches us to walk between these worlds. Not all pagan practices function at this depth of understanding. Many individuals practice and seek growth as they walk their path according to situations or circumstances that call for it here and there rather than as a way of life. The question of segregating the two realms is a moot point to the Medicine Woman. For the average person it becomes a choice to unite them as one, or as the modern Western mind frequently does, to keep them separate.

Hidden Truths Revealed Through Spirit

Some truths can be known, vanish, and be rediscovered or return proving their universal weight. Like an ancient grimoire that may be held by a master, it may be hidden at some point, and then resurface when it is most needed, when it is meant to do so...a mystery that only Spirit can manipulate. Truth stands on its own to repeatedly prove itself in some way, be it personal or empirical; it is never a supposition. Take the shaman and the Witch as an example. Personal truth for the shaman is that there is no delineation between the world of the mundane and that of Spirit. For the Witch, the world of Spirit must be tapped and contacted and the depth of the perception is varied. Does this mean that the truth is supposition? No. It is only that that truth works for one and not the other according to their perceptions of it. You have to get out and experience your spirituality firsthand to know it for yourself. The Medicine Woman will tell you that comes in the doing, in the experience of Spirit and yourself in union.

For myself, having experienced shamanic death, I know the truth of my own spirituality and in that I see the world as less complicated. Spirit showed me how I needed to simplify my life, showed me the clutter I needed to clear away so that I could proceed on my path unencumbered, and it lightened my heart. A void must be created if you are to fill that space with growth. A part of the quest is to discover the transformation as it progresses and leads us to the next encounter. We each have our own innate instincts that guide us to what we must do and experience. While there are differences between the genders, both men and women find that these instincts come naturally to one and thus become a struggle for the other. In the end, we both seem to come to the same or at least very similar insights. The more quests I complete, the clearer this becomes.

You do not have to compare yourself to others or what their truths might be in order to find your own. Trusting in Spirit to give you these answers and knowing that they will come is demonstrated in the results you get from opening to Spirit, and in the reception of Spirit's touch. Looking for validation in books and other places can be confusing and does not offer the evidence that is being sought other than to say another has experienced similar things. Only you can substantiate what your experiences are. The birth of a sunrise, the touch of Spirit, the wielding of the energy, the knowing firsthand a Spirit of Place, or working with the elemental spirits...all this and more cannot be captured and validated by anyone but you.

Seek your truths beyond what is written, then apply the knowledge you have gathered to make conclusions on your own rather than taking the word of others, so you can avoid a superficial structure. You must act to find truths beyond the written page, that is only a guide at best, an enhancement to the reality you are seeking, so that when you arrive at its door you will know to knock. Not knowing this beforehand, and arriving at the same door, you will find it still opens to you if your knock is persistent. This is why so many books offer exercises. The authors know that the only way you will understand is by experience, and they are trying to show you ways to do that. Just remember that the ways available to you are limitless.

Finding Spirit Through a Journey

Lessons come under many given situations or guises because all of us do not grasp them in the same manner. The truths of nature, the dimensional realms, and Spirit remain a constant. They are the same for everyone though we may agree or disagree on personal truths. That does not change what we know to be factual from personal experience. Open the first door if you will, but please do not become so caught up in the quest that you lose sight of the gifts you are being given. When you have a spiritual experience, it is a good idea to put it all down in detail. A journal is an excellent tool to follow your own progress and jar your memory as you move ahead. Details can often escape us as we can often become caught up in the process, and this is a good way to recall them. Writing the details down serves another purpose; it draws from you issues that you may have been overlooking while in a state of raised consciousness, little things that can later prove to be highly significant keys. It also helps commit the knowledge to memory. This is especially important when you first begin to enter into states of heightened awareness because it all seems to happen so fast.

One of my most poignant experiences came when I was allowed to see the shift take place and the awareness that another dimension had been entered...a portal being crossed. The scene around me was the same, but it shifted just slightly. It held a glow, a purity, a sharpness to it that is not there in the mundane world, and each blade of grass was as important as the next life-form; nothing was insignificant. It was breathtakingly beautiful and literally opened my eyes to visuals of what knowledge I had gained elsewhere. This can happen for you too, and when it does you know the meaning of splendor. You feel gratitude at the core of your being for the privilege you have been granted, and you give sincere thanks from the bottom of your heart. You will know when you have entered into such a state of consciousness. It will be felt in your spine, in your stomach, throughout your entire body physically as you sense a shift in the nature of your environment. You simply know when you have entered the sacred presence of Spirit.

There is a stillness that accompanies the moment of transition as a significant sign that change has taken place. The land speaks to you with the sounds of the location, and if you are careful to listen to the voices of the animals, plants, and rocks dwelling at that location, they tell you when you have been accepted. There is a scream of warning with any danger, or even when a spirit presence comes. The voices still at that moment as if to give honor to the presence of Spirit. Within the Medicine Wheel this same shifting of energy can be felt as you enter the different quarters. When your inner spirit is open, the boldness of the Guides becomes astounding. You may find yourself wishing you could stay there forever, but maintaining that heightened state of awareness is beyond the physical limitations of the mundane body. That awaits for the next world and the transcending of this one.

It is true that experience makes you more adept and the states of consciousness can be lengthier as time passes, but they cannot be maintained permanently. To walk between the worlds is to pick up on the subtle summoning of your Guides and Spirit, to open to them so the boldness can come through to you. There is deep pleasure felt in that. We can also indicate to Spirit and our Guides the ways we can best be reached. If you want a message to appear in some specific manner, you do need to search for it in an obvious fashion that will let them see you looking for it. They need to know the "address" you want to have your "mail" sent to so you can remain "informed." You can ask that it come to you through meditation, journeys, or dream work. A telepathic thought will come to you, a Guide will speak openly to you in a dream, a vision will be shown to you, a journey will take you into other realms; it is your choice. There are many watching points we can choose from and we have but to gaze or speak aloud to present our requests.

Tokens and Gifts

Often when such experiences take place and you are returning to the mundane you will discover a gift has been left for you from Spirit. That gift may be a stone, a feather, a staff, any number of things, but it will certainly catch your eye. It will stand out and call to you to claim it. These gifts become sacred items that we can use as tools to wield the lessons we have learned, for in them is contained the essence of that lesson. You must handle the items and summon that essence to surface within you. I always leave a token gift when I do shamanic work. It can be a crystal, a coin, a piece of bread, or a tobacco pouch. It is always something to say thank you for sharing with me, for the experience, for the transformation. Transformation always occurs to a greater or lesser degree due to the permeation of Spirit or guides passing into and through you. By touching you in spiritual ways, there is a piece of Spirit that remains with you always.

Completion of a Journey to Spirit

As I mentioned earlier, there is a time for rest when the assimilation process is completed. A time when an assimilation of the mystical euphoria passes and you need sleep. That may be extensive, lasting two to three times beyond what your normal sleep periods do. This is normal under these circumstances. You have asked a lot of your body and you have taxed yourself to new limits. In time you grow stronger at performing spiritual pathwork, but the sleep is always required. For the more quests and journeys you take the stronger the Medicine becomes, and there is always a testing to undergo. Your gifts become your strengths, but you always ask them to perform at maximal capacity when performing spiritual pathwork so you can enter deeper into the Otherworlds.

Your emotions range in extreme manners during these moments of Oneness, and that is taxing on your physical body as well. There then comes a period of rightness with the world and you know it has ended. Thus the sleep should be undisturbed and you should take measures to assure yourself of that. It may bring with it cementing dreams that confirm what you experienced or that polish off the raw edges of messages that may have left you hanging in limbo. Keep your journal handy, for when you awaken you will want to make sure to note any issues of importance...no matter how small.

It is truly exciting when you start to exercise the powers of your mind and heightened states of consciousness; it feeds the seeker within you, and keeps you to the path of finding Spirit. When I teach the Medicine to others it is to enhance the unfolding of each person's potential. You need to have the fundamentals of the Medicine Wheel, the Elements, meditation, visualization, and of spirits to understand your path and begin to walk them properly. (These fundamentals are discussed in detail in Part 2.) From this point, students naturally guide me to what they need by their questions and teaching me what to teach them. I do not know any other way of doing it. There are guidelines in books, but their understanding is really determined by the talents that emerge in the process and the interests that are held. I think that fundamentals and patience are the best things to teach...that and simplicity.

Keeping It Simple

Everyone wants to complicate things, to discover the big mystery, and we always think it is more than it is. People try to push the river and you just cannot do that. We all develop in our own time. The sooner the student realizes this fact, the better off she will be. We all need to learn to just let it come. You will feel more complete and have fewer negative experiences once you understand the need for centering, and experience the spiritual balance that allows healing to take place within you. You fill with the light and essence of Spirit, which acts as a shield to keep negative energies at bay. When you have allowed Spirit to enter into you, when you learn to embrace it, you will find you are healthier, happier, and more alert.

Finding your way to Spirit you come to know joy, essence, and fulfillment. A wise man once said: "So far as we have reason, we have the right to use it in determining what is right or wrong, and we should pursue that path we believe to be right." He was a chief and tribal leader called Black Hawk.

CHAPTER 8

THE SHAMANIC JOURNEY

A good friend of mine is a shamaness in Australia; her name is Lune, and she once said: "Shamanism, as I see it, is not a cultural practice. It is far too widespread throughout the different cultures and people of the world. Seeing this, it certainly seems that shamanism is a trait of humanity, not of one culture." These words were well spoken, and being of humanity it means that everyone can practice the pathwork of shamanism. The shamanic journey is part of that.

There are shamans found the world over and with them come symbols or keys that focus their intent and direct the inner spirit into dimensional worlds. A veil parts, allowing the practitioner to focus on another location outside time and space as the journey begins. The shaman can control where he goes, stop sound, stop action, control the speed of travel, and shift locations at the speed of thought. This journey is one into worlds of other beings and entities, where speech becomes telepathic. Movement is at will, and that intent allows the projection of the inner spirit to be accomplished.

Such a journey is never undertaken without the preparation of cleansing the mind, body, and spirit first. One must be in the proper state to enter if the experience is to be successful. Most conscious journeys start with breath control that directs the rate of our energy vibrations through the heart rate. Meditation focuses the attention and allows for visualization to occur. As the intent becomes focused through the will, the inner spirit awakens to project through trance or out-of-body experiences (often called shamanic flight) becoming mobile. By heeding the senses, the individual realizes they have become very acute in this state. Having proper intent and the highest of thoughts will attract like entities. If you possess negative thoughts or fears you will attract the lower level of entities (base entities without a higher purpose) that are a negative class. They are attracted to the energy in our life force, the spark that shines in the spiritual worlds. They are dark, brooding, and parasitic.

Warm sensations tend to be the higher entities, while the colder ones are the baser ones. This is true whether the experience is in the spiritual or physical realms of existence. During the process of the journey, the consciousness level is heightened and the awareness echoes spontaneous realizations. Later, when the traveler is experienced, they will find their Guide's voices often appear in the physical realm to help growth or summon them to receive a message. On this level there are both friends and foes, and it behooves the traveler to know the difference.

Journeys can be taken at different levels that vary from as little as a few minutes to hours. They include various states of trance, out-of-body experiences, and the projection of spiritual energy. All journeys are taken within the realm of Spirit, where entities are encountered who teach, guide, and protect the spiritual traveler. The baser ones will attempt to hold the traveler in their world and feed off the living energy that individual possesses. It is the higher entities that are sought, those that teach invaluable information about the various states of travel and wisdoms to be gained there.

Selecting a Space for Your Journey

With these things in mind, you will need to select the location for the work. It can be a sacred site where you might work with a Spirit of Place. These spirits do not usually leave their area of occupation, but they will teach or aid you, lending insight or powers on a temporary or permanent basis. None of this will happen, however, without the show of respect and honor they deserve. They dwell in a specific area as guardians of knowledge and have the ability to share it or withdraw it from those who approach them. I always address them as Grandfather or Grandmother as I sense their gender when they present themselves. There is a lot of confusion that rests in trying to name everything. By allowing all spirits to be Grandmother or Grandfather it simplifies matters initially. They are spirits and they do know our hearts. It is always advisable to leave a token offering with them. This can be tobacco ties, cornmeal, crystals, coins, a feather, bread, wine, or some other item of value to you.

The Voice of the Land speaks along with these spirits and you simply draw into nature deeper to unite with it and Mother Earth. The Voice of the Land is comprised of all sounds in localized areas to create its song, and these voices begin to speak to us in new ways.

Creating Sacred Space

After a purification ceremony I will go to a site where I plan to work and immediately lay out my offerings for the spirit I am calling upon. To do this and give thanks in advance leaves room to receive. The first step in creating a sacred space is the Medicine Wheel; be it in the air, laying out my pocket stones, or working with a physical structure on site. This is followed by a smudging of the area, which involves the burning of cedar or sage, allowing the smoke to purify the energies present. I center myself within the sacred space of the Wheel, joining in union with the Seven Sacred Directions as a part of that process. As I do, I become one with the elemental forces of Air, Fire, Water, and Earth. I become one with the Ancestors and Ancient Ones of the Below World. I become one with the Guardians and Teachers of the Above World. I become one with them all in the Middle World where I have become centered. At this point, I begin an introduction of who I am, why I have come, and if appropriate, ask to be announced to the greater spirit present there.

Entity Encounters

By centering and stilling the thoughts of the mind, it is possible to direct and release the inner spirit, thus slipping past the Veil of Illusion. Because Spirit is comprised of energy, and the inner spirit of the individual comes from this same source, the permeation through this veil into Otherworlds is readily accomplished. The entities often appear as luminous beings, filmy figures, or as lights. They can shapeshift and appear as different forms to different people. The relevance here is that they are teachers and will take you to different realms, share truths, and provide information through the telepathic links such a journey allows.

Encounters with these entities may well begin in the Dream Lodge, as this is where we are most readily able to accept them. Once the contact is made and experience has taken place, the individual progresses and may then enter the journey consciously through states of trance or projection to travel deeper. The teachers are capable of creating cosmic classrooms in which their lesson is given conforming to the specific needs of the practitioner.

Working with entities should be done with a mutual respect. They are not pets, nor are they beneath us. They are simply different, and deserving of respect. Do not presume a dependency on them. Their teachings are meant to show you methods, explain processes, and enlighten you so that you are better able to grow. When they have taught you what they came to teach they may stay or leave at their discretion.

Recognizing Blockages

If you are frustrated by not being able to advance on this path, you need to take time to examine your life from the present back until you find the reason for your blockage. This is not always easy to accomplish because it can often be very painful. Once the block is found, the obstacle is then torn down and you will be free to move ahead. You have to go back to a time when you put up the blocks to protect yourself, examine the incident, embrace it, and love it for the lesson it taught you, then release it. Your intent is perfected by using your willpower because they are one and the same. Your inner spirit will guide you initially as you free it from the physical body. You will hear it speak in your own voice, and your mind will accept it as its commander-in-chief.

When Spirits Appear

When I am alone with the ancient spirit, I open myself allowing it to read me. I hold nothing back; they are free to peruse all of me and see what I am about in every way. By stilling myself and sitting or standing quietly to listen, I will be told when I have been accepted or if it is better to leave. It is at this time that the spirit presence I have called upon will manifest in some fashion.

There are times I use tools such as my drum, rattles, or staff, but these depend on my purpose and the situation. There are times I am gifted and Medicine will be granted to me. These powers are not ours; they belong to Spirit. We are simply taught how to use that Medicine knowing where it may or may not be applied. Entering such a state is not done with expectation; rather, it is remaining open to accepting the possibility and that is when things happen. The spirits often challenge you before sharing their wisdom or gifts. These challenges are to be faced with courage, for that is what they are seeking to find in us.

Always remember you are but a channel for the power. So if fear does arise, you can summon the strength of Spirit to enter you and let you meet the challenge. Those who are just beginning or experimenting find that a general smudging and the right intentions will give them a glimpse into this type of journey and allow for some sort of experience to take place. It is through the journey that the shaman goes to learn ancient secrets, healing techniques, receive teachings, and explore the wonders that our own world only hints may exist.

The spirits that appear can be of the higher realms or relative to the Elements of Air, Fire, Water, and Earth. In the Lakota teachings, these Spirit Keepers of the quarters are Eagle of the East, Mouse of the South, Bear of the West, and Buffalo of the North. Their essence is of the Element that the particular animal represents. It is a process of learning to communicate with them, and once you have that concept in hand you are off and running. The shaman knows that the animals, the land, and the spirits all speak with a distinct voice. All of life talks to us if we learn to listen, and it is in this way that the poetry of the path can be heard. You can listen with your ears, eyes, mind, senses, or your emotions. The shaman will have learned to use them all. There is beauty seen, recognized, and honored everywhere.

The elemental spirits enjoy cooperating as you learn to work with your Medicine. By deepening the centering to journey into Spirit there is a sensation of walking through life with a sacred space surrounding you at all times. Acknowledging the energy present, the spirit of the trees, rocks, or a waterfall, these Grandfathers and Grandmothers become links to Spirit. All animal and local spirits are seen in this way and will at times accompany the shaman on a journey where an out-of-body shamanic flight takes place. They can and do read us, sensing our intentions, knowing if we have come for the right reasons, and responding to our thoughts.

Shapeshifting During Your Journey

We can at times shapeshift using the Medicine of any creature-teacher. Whether it is an animal we choose to call upon or our personal Totem, they bring a lesson or a message that will have serious meaning for us. We understand our Totems best because they mesh well with our nature and we are more attuned to them; however, any animal spirit can bring enlightenment. Those animals of perceived bad Medicine that come to us as a Totem teach us the responsibility or duty to overcome that negativity in ourselves. If a Power Animal holding the rank of a Totem also holds bad Medicine, it would be something we would tend to be in constant battle with as opposed to simply learning one day to overcome. The gift then is the awareness that we have the ability to shapeshift in our natures and we can take control over it.

When a Medicine Woman shapeshifts on a journey, she takes on the essence or spirit of that animal. There are tales of those who can do this physically, or of a change that will transform their countenance, but in most cases it is a shapeshifting of the spirit within us to that of the animal in question. I have not witnessed the physical change, but have seen the change of countenance, and others have seen it in me. In the case of shapeshifting, it is generally the ally that is called upon, though there are times when another spirit is invited into the shaman as well. Once it is accomplished we do literally become that entity, and there is the physical sensation of change taking place. We can then journey into Otherworlds, walk between them, run, fly, or swim through the realms in this new spirit form. We have its instincts, hungers, passions, and thoughts, and understand all of what is entailed in being that creature. By seeing life through its eyes, different perspectives are understood. Knowing its hunting patterns, survival skills, and nature removes the need to know why things are as they are. An understanding of the Medicine is reached, and with that we know how to put it to use.

How this power relates to our path, helps others, and serves Spirit allows for the growth we experience. It is power and wisdom gained through experience that is a great teacher in itself. Unlike the Guide that comes to reveal things, this is a firsthand encounter providing a greater scope of knowledge. In learning to shapeshift or journey as an animal, we learn more of what it is to be that animal, and how to incorporate it consciously by blending that power and wielding it. It is a gift from the Animal Spirit.

Once the shapeshifting has taken place, it becomes easier to do. If the animal is a Totem, it brings the realization that there is a right to call upon this power that has been granted. We can walk in the form of the unrelated spirit, gain some understanding, and perhaps even utilize its Medicine; but if it is relative to you then you share it always. Beyond this, the practitioner has the ability to summon that spirit from within and become it so he may journey in its form wielding its Medicine. There is an inner knowing and empathy with its nature and the clarity of recognition when the lessons are given. This is a very personal and powerful Medicine.

Many years ago these teachings were very deeply hidden, guarded jealously, and granted only to those perceived as worthy. People who wanted them had to fight to find them, and it often became a lifelong quest. They were seekers in the most intense sense of the word. The seekers still exist, but they seek in new ways linked to the old, and their battles are now levitating them as warriors from the mundane world into the realms of Spirit. More and more of this is changing, and what is coming about seems to be the natural order for Great Mystery as it unfolds, as much as a kaleidoscope has the ability to grant many visions in ever changing patterns.

Risks Exist

Through Power Animals or allies, the shaman comes to know the Guides that will teach and lead the way into Otherworld realms. However, there are also venomous or confining animals that can hinder an individual when they work with that Medicine. An experienced shaman will know that there can also be a transmutation of those negative energies and in smaller doses they become quite positive. Just as a small ingested dose of venom can become an antidote for a snakebite, or a small dose of a toxic plant becomes medicine to prevent pain or bring sleep, the practitioner learns to work properly with the risk factors. By drawing from the positive attributes and wielding the negative ones carefully, the transmutation for healing purposes is accomplished. The negative attributes are sought to be converted for positive results. Working in this context, the practitioner will draw from positive attributes and wield the negative ones carefully to accomplish the transmutation for healing purposes. Remember, a small dose heals; a larger one may kill.

Poisonous plants are much the same and the spirit that comes may offer to teach about the world of these green growing things. That knowledge must be kept in mind and questions asked relative to it. Judging doses can be critical and must be a constant issue when learning about them. The negatives must be overcome or tamed and that is the challenge the shaman sees on all levels. It takes a very balanced person to deal with the destructive aspects in relation to the risk factors, as in the case of an overdose or side-effect of nausea, vomiting, and hallucinations. These spirits will teach us how to become balanced. The person that has learned the secrets then becomes a very powerful individual, and her integrity is always being tested.

Changes Will Come

The years behind us have been painful growing years for humanity as a whole. It has come from its adolescence and into the adult phase of maturity and wisdom. I see the new millennium as ushering in yet another phase, that of the Ancient Ones returning: the wise ones, the Elders, those who will pass on the secrets to the world. What lies ahead is the maturity to recognize the wisdoms we have gained and the ability to wield them in utilizing our knowledge to its most beneficial purposes. It is something to look forward to with great optimism; it is a time that has been long in gestation, and the birth of a wondrous new age is at hand.

It is a time of change, foretold in the many prophecies—like that of the White Buffalo Calf. It is a time when cultures and races will begin to erase the lines of division between them and see humanity as a whole. It is a time when ancient wisdoms are being shared, when the consciousness of humanity is being raised to a new level of spiritual awareness. They are the forerunners to a new age of enlightenment—one where the dimensions begin to reunite with the physical realm we call reality and raise its values as well. The change is ushering in an era where our best qualities can shine forth. These words of prophecy can be seen in the emerging teachings of the Medicine Woman that have been long held silent. Grandmother Moon and Mother Earth are watching closely now. They see the rising force of women in the world. They see that a balance between the feminine and masculine has begun to take its place. It is time for this understanding, as women have danced the Medicine Wheel shuffling their feet for generations, that when one dance ends another begins. It is the time of a new dance. They know that when one door closes another will open, and the time for women's knowledge is now.

The Female and Male Journeys

We need to balance the masculine and feminine mysteries to create the wholeness and unity for the next generation of peace and transition. While the ways of men have dominated in the past, there are those among them that see the time for union is at hand. There are many who know the teachings of the male mysteries now seeking enlightenment into those of the feminine. It is as it should be. In understanding the process we can incorporate teachings from each other's ways to be in harmony with our own dual natures.

The bodies of women have always been ruled by the lunar tides; their mysteries come naturally to them; they reside within their wombs to tell them of life, death, and rebirth. They know that during the three days of their Moon Cycles there is a purging of the womb. This is the time they need to go within, to be alone, to commune with their inner spirits and become absorbed in that attunement. It is necessary to their spiritual growth and the understanding of their Medicines. The Moon Lodge of the Medicine Woman may be a dwelling apart from others where they can isolate themselves or an abode within their wombs themselves. It is there that we center, seek, and know the union. It is very necessary to our spiritual growth and understanding of our Medicine. This is the foundation of the Medicine Woman; it is the creative center...for all things are born of woman.

While the Medicine Men take an active role in coming to the male mysteries, they seek to possess them from outside themselves. They walk the land always searching, always reaching, always striving to grasp their Medicines. They quest, enduring the physical suffering that drives them out of their bodies into other dimensions where their answers lay hidden. Women's Medicine does not understand this need to explore and conquer themselves, though it does respect that it is the way of male powers. For women the mysteries lie within. Instinct, intuition, second sight—these things and more come to them quite naturally because they reside internally, and we work with them with the same ease as an inhaled breath of air.

The roles of the masculine and feminine aspects of our natures are different, and we come to know our mysteries wielding the Medicines that are ours. Men suffer outside themselves with physical pains that attack their bodies through the labors and other activities they perform. Women have their Moon Cycles, become impregnated, carry the child, endure the pangs of birth, and nurture life. It is enough for them and the ways we quest reflect this. It is the men who must suffer the physical pain of the ritual to gain enlightenment, but women have given their share already.

Journey to the Moon Lodge

The change that is taking place now is seeding the balance of both the masculine and feminine forces. A sprouting knowledge that we are gaining an insight to the other's ways is stirring the strains of harmony. We are the compliment of one another, not the enemy. Women carry the seeds of the next seven generations and the men seek them out to fertilize them. It takes both of us to guarantee the survival of the species. Together we are beginning to realize the truth of this and in the process raising the consciousness of the planet. We are the Dream Keepers and our children will become the Dream.

The secret of the Medicine Woman is found in the Moon Lodge each month. Mother Earth has taught us that there are 13 moons necessary for a complete cycle of the year to be achieved in her rotation. This is reflected in the Medicine Wheel stones that mark these 13 moons as taught to us by the Ancestors. The Wheel contains 36 stones in all. As women work through the Moon Lodge of the year, they focus on specific lessons in which each cycle or month is relative to a specific moon. The teachings are then culminated at the 13th moon and comprise a whole. The women know that a year and a day must pass before the next cycle of initiation can begin. It starts with the level of knowledge attained at that point and begins to grow from there. Each year brings greater understanding of these lessons and the forces they are working with. Each year is an initiatory period of growth and development in the mysteries of women. Through the teachings of Mother Earth and Grandmother Moon we come to know our wholeness in a process that brings about the transformation of our physical, mental, and spiritual bodies.

Each Moon Lodge we enter is a different lesson. Each lesson is one that leads to the next phase in the cycle. Each phase is in accordance with the path that the woman presents herself to. Enlightenment is achieved and wisdom is gathered. We are guided by Spirit, Mother Earth, and Grandmother Moon. We understand the rhythm of the cycles of life, the moon, and the energy shifts reflected in our bodies—the rhythm of the seasons where we learn to go with the flow. We see that we do not need to disrupt the natural order of things. We understand by going with the cycles and nurturing them we will move naturally into the next dance. While the women feel this innately within their bodies and inner spirits, men must outwardly seek to find such wisdom—they must see it and touch it to know it. Women already possess it.

Carlos Castaneda, in quoting the words of Don Juan Mateus, said: "Women are better than men in that sense. They don't have to jump into an abyss. Women have their own ways. They have their own abyss. Women menstruate. The Nagual told me that was the door for them." Don Juan's Nagual (spiritual teacher) had taught him that while men jump into the abyss of life to explore and discover its mysteries, women have an abyss of their own within themselves—the womb—and only women can understand it completely. Thus, men must find other ways of self-discovery. The differences between the ways of the Medicine Woman and the Medicine Man are in direct opposition to one and other and become evident once they are understood. Despite all their enlightenment and teachings, and although they may achieve similar results in their work, the methods that men use are different. It is for this reason that it can be said that men must seek their Medicine while women must open to theirs.

There are differences in the way men and women seek their visions as well. The women have been taught to prepare themselves differently from the men in this regard. Men must go out into the wilderness to seek their vision while the women enter the Moon Lodge to receive their dreams, visions, and truths. Women may also seek as the men do, but it is not as common for them. The need is not as strong due to their Moon Lodge teachings. While men traditionally fast and abstain from food or drink, women nurture their bodies with pure water and light foods. The vision quest of men demands sacrifice and giving of the self, while that of women is one of reception, fulfillment, and the impregnation of the inner spirit with enlightenment. Women come to know themselves in a deeply spiritual way; they understand naturally the rhythms that men seek to discover.

Women understand Mother Earth, come to know their Guides, and are guided in a gentle, innate fashion. They draw down Grandmother Moon and allow her into their wombs to impregnate their intuitions and instincts. They follow her to enlightenment. Men are mystified by both Mother Earth and Grandmother Moon feeling the pull, the allure, and the rise in their own emotional levels. They do not, however, know the sense of control over their emotions and wills that are akin to women's Medicine at such times.

A Time of Give-Away

Through both the shamanic journey and vision quest, I have been shown by Spirit that it is the time of the Give-Away. A time to give of yourself and your wisdom to others, which makes room for receiving other blessings. It is time for the Medicine Woman's teachings to be shared so that we may all become impregnated with the honor of union between the masculine and feminine. It is time to create a new harmony and balance that has been lacking for too long. We need to restore this state of equality through understanding the ways of the other and walking side by side, not one above and the other below. It will take an understanding of both paths to reach fulfillment, and the merging of the two to create the whole.

It will take the impregnation of the concept and the balance of these forces to give birth to the next generation, to heal Mother Earth, to walk our talk. It requires us to demonstrate the respect, honor, dignity, pride, and impeccable integrity within us. To do this well, it has become a time of doing for all. The harmony that must be achieved within each of us is the balance of the male and female principles, for they are within all our natures. It is the female principle of thought and the male principle of action, and we all think and act. Bringing our thoughts and actions into balance aligns these two principles and creates a state of harmony. It allows us to complete a cycle within each of us and move ahead to the next level of understanding. Without this knowledge it cannot happen.

In the teachings put forth today there is very little written that expresses the differences between the male and female roles. There is a difference between the path of the Medicine Woman and the Medicine Man, and though the two are often similar, there are variations in the way we perceive and actively carry out our roles. Much of what I have learned was from the male perspective of going "to" Spirit and "from" the body to achieve the gifts and succeed in wielding my Medicine. As a woman, this created a lot of confusion for me. Fortunately my Guides stepped forward to show me other ways.

The separation of male and female methods has always caused us to sit and shake our heads at the way our counterparts go about things. Women have known this but kept silent. This is the Medicine of Coyote, the Great Trixter who teaches through ironic humor. Coyote's lessons in life tend to come with frustration attached and conclude with humor generally found through hindsight. These lessons brought a perspective stemming from the way men and women seek only to discover the same things in the end using different methods. The Medicine of Coyote taught me to see things a bit differently. It occurred to me that just because I was a woman, and much of what I was able to learn was through a man's point of view, I could still benefit from the lessons if I just put a twist on them. I think this is an important issue for us all. Once we learn to achieve enlightenment in our own ways, we find the results of the information are the same and only the methods vary. As men and women we can learn from one another.

Through the teachings of women I came to realize that the female view helps women to recognize what is in us first before we can apply other methods (or parts of them) to what we already possess. While culturally, shamanic practitioners may have various traditional methods of communication, they are not at all that different once you learn how to figure them out. Today's expanded views and the ability to study these cultural variations enhances our ability to grasp the spiritual paths of others. It adds to our sense of heightened awareness, and it replaces prejudices with tolerance and respect. Success comes when we come to know we all walk a Medicine Path, and it is one of our own making, guided by our inner spirit. For the woman who chooses to walk this path, an understanding of the feminine principles is essential. In this way we will be wiser for the wear and better able to grasp the teachings of men and understand them. Because we both seek in different ways to find the same truths, by understanding the mysteries of women, the men will come to realize that there are things about women that compliment their ways and theirs ours.

I grew through trial and error time and again. Reaching an age of maturity as an Elder, I came to know that I am always in a process of completion. By no means have I achieved my full spiritual potential. There is ever growth to come. I have danced the Medicine Wheel and begun another round again for there are cycles within cycles, and I have journeyed through worlds within worlds. It is only understood by those who have walked this path to the point of recognizing when one dance leads to the next in its subtle transformations. For many the full potential of their Medicine is achieved in mid-life when there is time to devote to the workings. We all have our own time frames, and it is unfair to compare ourselves to those of others.

In our own ways, we women and men come to the same conclusions, the path that takes us there is the difference. Accepting this truth then is the first step to discovering that we can work differently side by side. It teaches us that we can achieve a balance that will allow for harmony to displace the battle of the sexes that has waged throughout history.

A time is at hand to end that war in peace, to create a union of strength through harmony and honor the ways of others. Those who feel the twinges of jealousy or fear the paths of others will need to become enlightened. It is a choice of which way you will walk and what you will take upon your path with you. I choose to walk balanced in the center and know the One-ness, to walk between the worlds—all of them. I choose to be a part of that change, even if it is only a feather in the wing that lifts us to the heightened awareness before us. This too is part of the shamanic journey.

Whether we journey in our minds, out-of-bodies, or on our paths, each method reaches out to us with enlightenment and understanding that helps us to grow into that which we already are. It is a process of Be Com-ing, and learning to work in the ways that we are best suited. Each of us has the ability to journey in some form, and the longer we walk our paths the more ability we attain, allowing us to sample what is available to us. We may not all be able to shapeshift initially, but when we understand the process and see that it reaches into all aspects of our lives, the concept begins to seed itself. When we can see it growing through our actions, we come to realize that we can take those actions to other aspects of our be-ing. That is when we realize that shapeshifting is a reality, that we can trans-form ourselves, physically, mentally, and spiritually. It is then that we have found the method to reach deeper and the transformation into our Spirit Guides, Totem Animals, or Power Animals is no longer such a preposter-ous image; it, too, becomes reality.

The shamans of Australia shapeshifted and visited one another, leav-ing a sampling of their soil. In doing this others knew when they had been through their territory. All traditions have their own way of notifying other practitioners of their presence. Worldwide there are geoglyphs and mark-ings that depict areas of sanctity and are the suspected markings of shamanic pathways. Here in the United States, we have some of our own signs of passing and markers to follow; there are others that are universal. Some signs are mingled with the past and some with the future. Shamanically speaking, there are many ways to communicate travel and location and who is visiting whom. There are journeys yet to be taken and flights of wonder to know. Upon these journeys the energy of Spirit and the universe can be seen radiantly aglow. Like heat waves rising from hot surfaces in the summer, these waves are energy, and like them, all else radiates its own aura. Some see energy in shades of clear to black, some see colors, and others feel it in degrees of hot or cold sensations. A journey cannot be taken without something being learned from it, and in that learning we come to a greater depth of wisdom that reaches far into comprehension and away from words.

It is up to each of us to decide if we will come to know such a journey. It is up to us to choose how far we will explore the possibilities, making them our own experiences, and therefore our own reality. Life is the illusion, and it is up to us to lift that veil. It is only then that we may begin to prepare ourselves for the dance of the vision quest and yet another reality. Meanwhile, there are endless shamanic journeys to be made, and you have only to open to yours and your own style of achieving it.

CHAPTER 9

VISION QUESTING

Come, be comfortable, sit. I am going to pass you the Listening Stick as I share with you the mystery of the vision quest. It is said that on some nights the Wolves are silent and the Moon howls. It seems quite appropriate to relate this to the quest because this is where a shamanic death of the inner spirit takes place...a sometimes bittersweet and painful experience as the old aspects of self pass away. The process is followed by an amazing spiritual rebirth in the loving grace of Spirit's embrace. While people seek for many things in life, the vision quest appears as an integral part of Great Mystery. This quest comes as a summoning from Spirit and is the driving force behind discovering the ways of the Medicine Paths.

As a Native American tradition, it is one in that a person learns to open, become internally cleansed, and to be renewed. Through laughter, tears, and silence the true joy of stepping into the future can be known. A call from Spirit gives the permission to quest. Offering a new worldview, it brings with it a sense of purpose, a defined path, a prophecy, or some life-altering transition of great importance. This means the call must be legitimate, and to find such truths you must be willing to undergo the trials a search like this entails. The summoning can be brought to your attention in a wide variety of ways, but it is always from the core of your being that you sense it taking root and growing intensely. With great anticipation for what lies ahead, new vistas begin to open and the work that is to be done becomes a highly passionate quest in itself.

Receiving the Call to Quest

The call of the quest can be initiated through a journey, vision, from an animal or Spirit Guide, a Dream Lodge experience, or in some other fashion. The questor feels drawn to communicate directly with Spirit in a very intimate way, and through that intimacy becomes enlightened. Those who know of the call will pray when it first comes so they will know it is a true summons and that they have been given permission to quest. The methods practiced from this point on will vary depending greatly on the tradition followed or knowledge available. There is always a choice to answer or refuse.

It is quite common to take this information to the local shaman after praying. At that point the individual undergoes readiness and counseling. For those who practice outside the traditional ways, it is an independent issue that requires them to cry prayers and take on the risks involved. If it is done in ignorance, there can be obstacles to success due to improper purification or preparation. For this reason, intense study on the processes involved is necessary so opening to Spirit is understood and guidance can be accepted naturally.

The quest is a linking to the Creator as the state of consciousness begins to shift higher. A channel opens between the individual and Great Mystery while the mundane world slips away and is eventually left behind. To an outsider this may seem to be an obsession, but to those who know it is a very determined focus that initiates the growth of the spirit. No one willingly undergoes this experience just for the fun of it...it is very serious business. The quest reveals the purpose of life for each individual, why the particular path is being walked, and who is to be served. Choosing to respond to the call is exciting and carries with it some trepidation.

The Stages of Questing

Whether or not the call is heeded depends on you and your ability to meet such a life-altering challenge. It requires a sense of self and the courage to face the unknown. Following the call there are four stages that complete the vision quest: fasting, purification, isolation, and assimilation. Each of these stages can last from one to four days or more. While it works well for those who are seeking the path of a shaman, and for some as an ideal (because some people wait a lifetime to have such a vision), time does not always allow for such elaborate proceedings. This is especially true when the individual is not a shaman and the demands of the mundane exist.

Often those who are working independently prefer to respond with a shorter version. The time frame would be divided into four equal parts to accommodate their requirements. Spirit does understand the need for the shorter versions and I have had good success with them. They may include consecutive nights of extensive Dream Lodge work, or require a follow-up quest to complete the entire process, but in either case success does come. The depth and scope of the longer version cannot be expected to be achieved this way, but the shorter quests are always enlightening and life altering.

Stage One: Fasting

The method of preparation is always at the hand of Spirit in one form or another. If guidance is needed Spirit will do so or provide a shaman to act as a mentor. In the first stage the questor fasts in an isolated location to purify the mind. This is done either alone or with a shaman who follows the same rigors and sets the pattern to be emulated. This is a time of examining blockages and the path being walked. The duration of the first stage lasts anywhere from one to four days depending on the depth of the vision being sought. These first days allow the individual to begin making an initial shift in perceptions as the mundane draws back into the shadows. The fasting also serves to prepare the body for the second stage of the process by eliminating impurities.

An Inner Search for the Call

The initial call is examined in depth. A shaman will decide through an interview process if it is a true call or wishful thinking, thus determining if they are willing to guide the questor through the rigors that need to be followed. The path that leads to this quest is one filled with self-discovery, and the pitfalls are those barriers that are built in life, the ones people bury and forget. It is the task of the shaman to help seekers delve into their own psyche and draw forth memories; to face fears and confront them; to come to know their own courage. This is not an easy process because it requires time and effort as confrontations are not always initially apparent. Some obstacles are placed there, as my dear friend Advent says, "By intent and habit"; thus most people tend to overlook them. The process of discovering what these obstacles are requires that they be seen as walls erected to hide pain, remain safe, and forget.

It is essential to know the shadow self and that the pathway the quest leads to will present the consequences of that action in the quest. The integration of insight and understanding gained through shamanic lessons allows the inner spirit to come forward in the sense of conscious awareness of its presence. Then reintegration takes place as we learn to consciously work with our inner spirit on a new level. The lessons are about confronting the self always in one form or another. The blockages come when we deny truths about ourselves or life. Then we have to confront them to grow along our paths of spiritual evolution. It is a part of the process of soul retrieval. It is the wisdom that allows the shaman to assist in the removal of blockages, demonstrating that these issues can be embraced. By finding the pieces of the shattered soul or to the individual's problematic issues and helping the questor to reintegrate them in a right way of thinking, the process allows unity to take form. Through love and acceptance the lesson is embraced, and the blockage brought forth is acknowledged. By tearing down old misconceptions, a sense of wholeness manifests. New truths are revealed producing a healthier mind, body, and spirit, integrating an emergence on both inner and outer levels.

Many people need to realize that to fight for our inner spirits in one way or another is asked of all of us. As the process unfolds, the shaman will explore the relationship of the individual to her social environment. By looking for the keys that point out where the blockages lie, the individual learns to recognize the method and patterns of his life. The questor is helped through various levels of transition and interpretations of what has happened.

When a shaman personally experiences numerous quests, he or she becomes a highly qualified shamanic guide who can discuss issues in great depth. It allows the shaman to recognize who is ready and who is not through the establishing of intimacy and perfect trust. To do a total soul retrieval, the shaman and the questor must achieve union at a mutual point. For this reason the shaman sacrifices and endures the rigors right along with the questor. A spiritual balancing and centering at a conscious level brings about the initial unity. It allows for understanding, empathy, respect, and a teaching of the ways that will permit new strength and confidence to be achieved.

Through persuasion of the questors' inner spirit, the shaman helps them to regain self-respect, dignity, and honor. The centering deepens and harmony feeds the restoration or healing in as unobtrusive a manner as possible. We all have deep secrets that we want to keep buried, wounds that are too painful to recall, and fears that require more courage than we think we have to face them. That fear alone is enough to prevent a successful quest. In exposing themselves to Spirit it is discovered that whatever was done, was done to the whole. If the questor can see that, forgive themselves and the errors of their ways, or learn from the deed, then they will be able to vow to Spirit that it will never happen again.

The same applies to any injustices suffered by individuals. They will know in their hearts that this is true, because they will have sincerely learned a lesson that was meant for them. The understanding brings about a change within the questor initiating the first stages of a spiritual rebirth. A choice is made to trust in Spirit with more of the self than has ever been given before. That takes a lot of courage.

Spiritual Reintegration

Part of the reintegration process requires journey work to see what needs to take place in the path of the questor. This is done by the individual or occasionally with the shaman in a mutual journey where the shaman enters into the spiritual dimension to commune with the individual's spirit. The shaman's task is to educate the person who has come before them. The purpose of this soul retrieval is to aid the individual in the recovery of pieces that have been torn away. The questor must learn to reunite these pieces with the aid of their inner spirit through acceptance and tearing down of old misconceptions.

All of us experience blockages that need to be faced from time to time. They show us our weaknesses and gift us with our strengths. It takes the pain of what we must face to strike the chord within us, a process that is not easy, but if it were, there would be no significance or value to it. Putting forth the effort allows for growth, for experiencing the issues one last time, an ability to break them apart, to take back that piece of ourselves lost or surrendered out of fear, trauma, or abuse. The Medicine People know from their own experiences that shamanic death is repeated at each major stage of growth. For those that seek the shaman and do not walk the path per se, it is perceived as simply a healing session. The shaman, on the other hand, sees it on a much deeper spiritual level, guiding them to the resolutions they are seeking.

During the time of fasting, counseling, praying, and working through issues, there are more mundane distractions that are taking place. The sacred grounds are being prepared for the vision quest and the Sweat Lodge is erected. While physical labor is at times strenuous, the tasks are simple in nature, providing freedom of the mind to ponder. This allows the sorting out of all necessary issues as the logical mind filters the spiritual nature of what is happening to accept it.

Stage Two: Purification

The Sweat Lodge is a structure made of young saplings in a domed style similar to an igloo. The saplings frame it and canvas, fabric, or hides covers it. There is a sense of creating something in the building of the Sweat Lodge. It symbolizes Mother Earth, thus to enter is to seek being born anew in some fashion. So it is called the Mother Lodge by some tribes. It is a place of purification, of being spiritually reborn, to speak to the Spirit Helpers, request visions, seek enlightenment, and pray for others. It is the symbolic womb of Mother Earth.

The Stone People dwell there, and the Sacred Fire of Spirit is made ready. The Stone People are the rocks used. All that exists is seen to have life in it. These stones form a pit to hold the Sacred Fire or Spirit—the Fire that Spirits or Guides will enter through or utilize. It is a pure element and Spirit dwells within it. This fire represents the creative force in life. It is on the order of a sauna in that rocks are heated and the participants sweat out impurities. The difference from a sauna is that this is a spiritual or religious focus considered to be very sacred. Being a symbolic womb of Mother Earth, it is entered in reverent ritual fashion. In the purification of the quest area, the sacred grounds are made ready to accept the questor. These tasks, when completed, signal the end of the first stage and beginning of the second, the Sweat Lodge itself. The individual enters the Lodge to purify the body and inner spirit while bringing about a more integrated state of consciousness. Symbolism begins to take on a new depth of meaning during the sequestering.

Any physical suffering encountered in the Lodge demonstrates to Spirit what the questor is willing to endure in order to be worthy of the vision being sought. It is at this time a sacrifice will be determined if it is not yet known. Spirit messengers of various kinds are known to appear in the Mother Lodge, revealing things pertinent to the path walked or the quest itself. Through those insights and issues an elation is achieved. An Otherworldly shift takes place, and the next cycle of the dance begins.

Stage Three: Isolation

The third stage begins when the individual enters prepared grounds with the bare essentials to sustain him or her during the stay. At this point total isolation is necessary. The questor will smudge and center before offering up the proper sacrifice and then begin prayers and a meditation process. Should the vision come early in this phase, the questor will remain isolated for the duration of the pledge, aware of the need not to break the oath that is taken prior to questing, which states the duration of time the questor is willing or able to commit to the quest. Sometimes more will be revealed and the visions come in stages of their own.

Those who quest do so for extended periods of time until the vision comes or until they are unable to sustain themselves, demonstrating their strength of endurance and dedication. They present a giving of their personal essence to Spirit and are usually undertaken by the ceremonial leaders who remain isolated for a month or more. The vision quest takes the individual deeply into the realm of Spirit far beyond the boundaries of the shamanic journey. Heeding this call allows one to grow in areas that are otherwise inaccessible, teaching the capacity to which that individual will be expected to serve.

The Site for Stage Three

The location for stage three of the quest site is generally out in the wilderness where there is exposure to the elemental forces. A fair amount of physical discomfort may inundate the questor, and the entities that stray into the area are kept at bay by sacred space and perhaps a fire. Such questing sites can be a waterfall, atop a mountain, in a cave, on a hilltop, at a sacred site, in an energy vortex, in a Medicine Wheel, or simply in a place where a hole has been dug simulating the grave and womb of Mother Earth from which the questor will emerge.

A few ritual tools and supplies may be brought to the site, including a Sacred Pipe, tobacco, drums, rattle, flute, smudge pot with herbs or a smudge stick, water, a pocket Medicine Wheel, and of course any token offerings that are to be presented to the spirits. There is often a fire pit prepared and a blanket to sit on or cover up with at night. During this time very little, if any, food or drink is taken depending on the tradition followed.

Piercing the Flesh

In the Lakota tradition, men who quest often make a sacrifice by piercing their flesh. By tethering to a tree from their breast, or to a buffalo skull that is dragged behind them from their shoulder blades, they endure a great deal of physical suffrage. The women may offer a sacrifice of skin cuttings, though some will occasionally pierce their skin. When done properly, the questor feels minimal pain if any. It is done to demonstrate the intent, endurance, and strength of the individual involved, and is considered to be the ultimate sacrifice one can make. To prevent infection from setting in, the pierced areas are treated with special herbs prior to and during the endurance period.

I have not chosen to pierce in my quests, but I have experienced other tests that demanded mental, emotional, and physical strength to be summoned from the very core of my being. Not all quests are so taxing, and those of the Moon Lodge show a very gentle side where Spirit allows women to discover that there are sacrifices we make as a part of life. Those sacrifices bring about allowances for our efforts and intentions as well. Women have the ability to conceive, carry a child, give birth, and nurture life. Great sacrifices are made at such times, and with them come the pain of mind, body, and spirit. For the woman this is considered enough to give, though many individuals feel they should offer more and do.

The sacrifice is always something that is proper to give up for our own benefit, and we are expected to hold to that offering. It can involve skin piercing, cuttings, yielding up of old negative habits, or making some other major change in life. I know that if we follow our own path and techniques, Spirit will teach us and tell us what we need to do when our intent is demonstrated in the right manner.

Women's Medicine is considered very powerful because all things are born of woman; thus, when an offering to add her skin cuttings to anything is made, the essence of her Medicine is incorporated, and the power of the item is seen to grow in strength. Some men tend to fear the Moon Time of women. It is a time when they are closest to Grandmother

Moon and Mother Earth, a time of linking great powers. Women are enmeshed in the flow so intensely that their very presence can disrupt the workings of others. They understand this mystery while men do not always receive such teachings, though in time they can come to have great respect for it as they comprehend the theory.

A woman who is not trained to work in the Moon Lodge is subject to wide swings in her moods and temperament, which is where dangers lie. With these often raging hormones and emotions come fits of temper, careless words, and sometimes reckless actions. Those who know better pull away socially using that time for spiritual growth. This allows for focusing and balancing the energies in order to utilize them for their most positive aspects.

The Vision

Isolation provides the individual with the time and space necessary to be alone with Spirit, so that recognition can take place and the vision received will, as a rule, relate directly to the individual. The vision tends to clarify their purpose in life and how they are to serve Spirit. It can define a path, a service to the community, clarify abilities, gifts, powers, or any number of other issues. Many times prophecy will be involved. Any gifts received, such as healing tools, plants, or songs of power are considered sacred and honored as such. When isolated, they will remain to cry for a vision, to pray, and call for it from the heart. The one seeking must want it so badly that she is willing to express all that is within her through her passionate emotions in order to obtain this vision. They will dance, drum, sing, cry, and call for the vision in every way available.

The gift for facing the deep truths within us and trusting in Spirit is the granting of a vision. Slipping mundane boundaries and lifting the veils to other dimensions, Spirit becomes known. The Medicine Wheel may be danced as the spiral takes the questor upon a path that is one of a kind. The waiting is often the hardest part for many people, because it is natural to be anxious for immediate results. The vision comes through a heightened state of awareness as one begins to see beyond normal ranges of perception. The barriers of time, space, and dimension are broken. Often trance states of altered consciousness are experienced. The questor may journey to meet a Spirit Guide, enter the Dream Lodge, or the clouds may open up to reveal a scene from an event that has already become a part of history.

The event will need attending to in some way, either as a message or prophecy to take back to the people. It will involve the questors and their future actions to some extent and may include astounding visions of prophecy depicting social, cultural, or world changes. It can appear super-imposed on the environment, or a rend in the very air itself can open revealing dimensional shifts. Spiritual beings may enter, exit, or lead through veiled portals. Transformation takes place along with the shift. It is quite common for the questor to experience shapeshifting, out-of-body flight, and a wide variety of other phenomena. What is revealed can be awesome or frightening to see. It can be a vision that inspires pathwork or one that portends activism to prevent a crisis or catastrophe. The insights granted allow comprehension exceeding the range of normal abilities, and as it peaks the questors suddenly understand many things and "get the message."

For those who seek to become shamans or Medicine People, the vision usually contains important information that pertains to the needs and leadership of the people whom they serve. They will be shown their Medicine and often given special gifts such as herbs, songs, chants, dances, and ceremonies. These same visions can be highly personal, and then a broader view of how it plays in the world is made known. Spirit allows you to glimpse the world from such an elevated perspective that you feel you can see all.

Expect the Unexpected

Even when you go to the vision quest prepared you never know what will happen. Some shamans are gifted with the ability to journey from a distance and observe what the questor has seen, which is of great benefit during the assimilation period. It is for Spirit to know and decide what you will be granted and for what purposes. During one of my own quests, Spirit showed me that it is the harmony of life we need to be seeking and that I should share my knowledge of the Medicine Path with others. I was told to become a bridge for others to cross upon. This has become the purpose of my path. The teachings I share are to help others find their own spirituality, not mine, but their own link to Spirit. We all must walk our own paths. With the vision comes a transformation that washes over you, and you feel the touch quite literally. It is so very moving, often gentle like a feather or whispered breath that sweeps you clean. It can also be highly dramatic and hold you transfixed in awe just as easily. It can be like a rushing wind or the full impact of a merging spirit that bowls you over and knocks you off your feet. It always comes with the love of Spirit and the feeling of grace that love possesses.

While the quest will test every fiber of courage, strength, and endurance the individual possesses, new fears must be worked through as they arise in this isolated state. Remember there are very real risks involved because this is a wilderness area exposing the individual to the elements and wild animals. It is here that the questors seek to find a purified union with Spirit and if a state of trance comes over them there are vulnerabilities. While most wild animals are kept at bay by a fire or simply sensing this moment with Spirit and honoring it, there is no guarantee.

Gifts received may be in the form of powers of enlightenment, prophecy, healing, tools of Medicine, or the ability to see beyond the mundane world. They can be items of power or ways of using cosmic energy that are compatible with your own nature. During the quest you will be shown how to use them and receive a lesson. You will also demonstrate your understanding. Always the vision and gifts are appropriate to you and the path you walk.

Shamanic Death

Birth itself is a painful process demanding all of the mind, body, and spirit that an individual can give. Shamanic death is alluded to in many teachings as a spiritual process of rebirth. Along with right intent, the shaman's death is the willingness to complete the process of the vision quest. It is the willingness to have every nook and cranny within you examined for all its light and shadow. It is the desire to be reborn into a better, stronger, more stable spirit. That can only happen when you face Spirit alone and sincere. It happens when you say: "Spirit, I am ready and open completely. Hear me as I speak. Touch me as I am. Make of me what you will."

Wholly giving yourself to Spirit is a cosmic experience. Fear of death is lost because the embrace of Spirit is experienced as everpresent; doubts fade and truths received are unquestionable, allowing for perfect trust. Once shown these realities, renunciation of them becomes the ultimate lie. Knowing these things as facts of life, the questor pays close attention and vows to do his part. Remember that Spirit loves you in such a profound way that there is nothing that cannot be forgiven if you are willing to do the same for yourself and others. There is nothing that cannot be healed if you are willing to be healed. There is nothing that will not be shown if you are willing to see and accept it. Spirit literally steps in and washes you clean, leaving a sense of purity, refreshment, newness. This embrace is the experience behind the shamanic death and rebirth. This is soul retrieval at its pinnacle.

In my experience, I have found shamanic death comes in a brief moment when Spirit confronts us with knowledge and we realize that we have a choice to yield up our robe or to continue living. It is very profound as the decision is made consciously at the core of our being. The inner spirit decides and there is no logical mind standing in the way to argue. It is just done and we stand in the afterglow knowing we will keep our word.

As you walk back into mundane reality the presence of Spirit appears to withdraw to attend other matters, but you know a part still remains. Accepting this openly, the state of heightened awareness shifts once more. Lessons may continue at this point or you may find that the quest is winding down somewhat. As it slows down there is a state of bliss that washes over you. Those who have been watching in silence will recognize that it is safe to approach the individual and assist them in returning to the shaman.

For the independent questor there is simply time spent alone. At first you cannot sleep. There is so much running through your mind and such wonder in your heart that your energy is soaring. Even after grounding yourself, the residual of Spirit's touch, the comprehension of the vastness of the union you have experienced is overwhelming. So you laugh, or cry, or sit silently. You remain to let it all simmer down in a gradual process. There is a euphoric feeling of buoyancy where all is right with the world. You feel as if you could levitate, and you really do not want to be around others at the moment. Then mundane reality slowly seeps back in, the euphoria gradually passes, and you realize that it is not humanly possible to maintain such a state indefinitely.

At this point a heaviness comes and you begin to want sleep. That period of sleep is usually lengthy and may last up to 24 hours or more. The quest deprives the individual of rest and asks a lot of the body, which has its own demands by now. During this time there may be dreams of great importance. You will not forget them easily, but it is advisable at that time to share them with the shaman for extensive interpretation or to write them down in a journal because the world is about to close in on you again.

Stage Four: Assimilation

There is a filtering process that takes place with a journal acting to create a link between your conscious mind and your inner self as you begin the final assimilation stage. A time of continued sacrifice begins with a modified fast when the sleep has ended. Only light meals of pure foods are taken. These foods are "alive" with spirit: raw vegetables, fruits, grains, nuts, berries, and occasionally certain sacred meats. This is to restore proper nourishment to the body gradually, show homage for the success of the quest, and to acknowledge the path before you.

These next few days are a quiet time as the assimilation back into society is put off for just a bit longer. Most are consumed with thoughts of elevated awareness and spiritual proportions. Words do not adequately fit the experience. Only one who has shared something similar can begin to comprehend what you are trying to convey. Such thoughts should not be shared with those less experienced. They would not even begin to understand...you are still trying to do that yourself.

In the aftermath of vision quest this heightened state cannot be maintained either. You must return to your logic and the conscious mind cannot take your experiences all in right away. All that has happened must sink in and rise to the surface again gradually. This process takes time as you work it all into your worldview and see where the pieces fit into your now reborn spiritual persona. It is a settling of the knowledge, enlightenment, and the gifts of Spirit.

The powers that you have received are held in great honor. If you are working with a shaman you may be asked to demonstrate them or you may desire to do so on your own. Beyond this they will never be flaunted in public because it would dishonor you and Spirit. After undergoing all this to achieve your blessings, you should not be willing to throw them away so easily.

Individuals undergoing the process repeatedly have very strong abilities to wield their Medicine. According to the Plains tradition, quests are undergone in sets of four to reach four different levels of initiation onto the shamanic path. There is at least a year between the quests, so at the very least, it takes the shaman a minimum of 16 years to complete. The vision quest becomes a lifelong journey of growth and enlightenment cycles. With the gifts of power come the responsibility of wielding them well. It is done without question, to serve Spirit and society as a whole.

While it is true that the gifts received are often applied to the needs of the shaman, such actions are not the main focus. The shaman's needs, however, do help lead the questor to ways in which he may be of service to others. Being a shamanic leader requires the ability to know the fine lines that define those actions. Altogether the traditional vision quest is a process that takes just over two weeks to complete. While what takes place is a gift in itself, it tends to begin to fade in time.

The need to stay connected to that new part of yourself and separate from the mundane world residually goes beyond the quest to a daily and even moment to moment issue. It often continues throughout one's life (tracing the shadow of the quest), though not all who quest take it to such extremes. Those who enter once are changed to some major degree, those who enter repeatedly become continually transformed. The gifts must then be honed and in that process testings will come at the hands of Spirit.

Testing

Such testings can include temptation to show off, new blockages, trials of confidence, challenges by spirits, or changes in mundane life. Some may challenge you by saying that you are walking a path not meant for you. These are all challenges to enlightenment and wisdom. It is up to you to face these, demonstrate your capabilities where they apply, and move ahead on your path.

Quest of the Shaman

Each quest brings a new depth of understanding that is reached. It is for this reason that the Sioux shamans undergo 16 major quests. Such an achievement is never easy, and many never reach those final stages. However, it is the goal of the shaman to seek all stages before finally dropping their robes.

For the Medicine Woman, the vision quest becomes broken into smaller stages each Moon Time. That means that there are 13 quests undertaken each year building to the culmination and new cycle that continues the process. For the Medicine Woman, it is always ongoing and the growth is a continual process...a flow into spiritual maturity. Regardless of the number of quests completed by the shaman or shamaness, it is the quest of the moment that is always most important.

The Now is faced by completely opening up to it, learning to fully channel cosmic energy at will. As long as the intent and purpose are right, there is never a backlash. Fear is simply the manifestations of things within us needing to be brought to the surface, challenged, and transformed. This is not done with a careless flip of the hand, but with long careful examinations. In facing fears you place your trust in Spirit to right them. It is the fear of the unknown that rears its head at this point. No one knows exactly what will happen, what entities will appear, what they will do or how they will choose to challenge. No one knows how they will react and a constant state of courage is required.

Sharing Your Quest

You will instinctively know whom to share your experience with. When you are able to share it there is an initial excitement and tendency to want to spill forth with details. I think this is because you realize that the person you are opening up to understands and honors the things you are saying. We learn to adapt to the process itself as time passes. As other quests are undergone, this need to share all with your confidante seems to dissipate considerably. The subsiding of that need does not lessen the importance of what you have undergone, but simply serves to express the growth you have achieved. The eagerness to communicate details passes, but the enlightenment is exchanged when the appropriate time presents itself (which usually happens with equally or better qualified people).

When a quest has been successful and someone else shares with you their own experiences, you feel blessed to have had such an honor bestowed upon you. You know what it took for them to accomplish it, and they are often gifted with a form of enlightenment in the process. When two experienced people discuss questing, the interpretation process takes on a slightly more intense focus. They are able to delve even deeper into the meanings of the symbols and impart perspectives to one and other. The level of trust between such friends is amazing, and it allows for even greater sharing, for nothing is held back. It also speeds the assimilation process and is quite rewarding with its insights. Such sharing is a source of support and confirmation because they enjoy a camaraderie that is quite unique.

Once the gifts are received you will grow into them, be tested on them, and either pass or fail. If you fail, the gifts will obviously take longer to master, but it does come. If you pass, a new cycle of initiation into even greater mysteries begins. The testing is another door to another initiation or quest, but you are always given a choice, given freewill to decide if you will accept or reject the offer. Any deceptions that have taken root in you at the time are confronted as new fears, barriers, or issues to be faced. You must cleanse before you can accept again. The pattern continues but by that time much of the initial fear is gone and the sanctity of the rite is consuming.

All this and more awaits upon the Medicine Path, which begins by entering the Silence where shadows hide and answers reside. Understanding the process brings about an inner sense of freedom when you know that the light of Spirit burns within us. Its heat is the heat of the living body. When we walk with proper intent, with impeccable integrity, we are walking with Spirit and therein resides the key. We cease to serve the whole and maintain our link when we give into our own authority and take it personally. We become self-serving.

Remembering that leadership is service to others regardless of who is following behind allows us to maintain proper thought and intent keeping our integrity intact. All too often the cares of the mundane world, with all its ills, blind those in positions of leadership to this truth. They fall prey to the illusion they begin to create. It is the shaman who strives to always know the difference, who resides in the Now of the moment that succeeds in serving All Our Relations.

Shamanic Reality

Some never do experience shamanic reality or the spiritual enlightenment such a path presents. The events that take place in the world of a Medicine Person reach far beyond the physical reality of a mundane life. These events, being of a spiritual or Otherworldly nature, add to the rich tapestry each shaman weaves. The events are set into motion alongside phenomena that do not follow the laws of the physical reality most people know. The Shaman does not see the physical and spiritual as separate realities, but as a united whole where the unusual is understood and commonplace. When this happens, that shaman has begun to solve a small piece in the riddle of Great Mystery. It is a view that has found acceptance through the shaman's personal experiences. It thus becomes a sacred and spiritual reality. While the average person may see these events as flights of fancy or even unusual isolated incidents, the shaman lives them, and takes active participation with them. In the process insights are gained that would not otherwise be grasped. This insight is a direct result of communion with the Creator, Spirit Helpers, Teachers, and Guides from other dimensions. There are endless messengers sent to us from Spirit and they wear many guises. The shaman knows them well. We cannot judge those whose paths have not brought them to shamanic reality. We can certainly choose to respect the ones they are on and see that we need not walk them any longer. It is my firm conviction that once you come to know Spirit such a path is illuminated beyond comparison, and walking that path is a privilege. You will have found your spirituality no longer doubting if it is right or wrong. When others ask you to explain yourself you will hold your answers. You will be able to walk your talk with namaji: with respect, honor, dignity, and pride.

Never discount your efforts to succeed. Spirit is always aware and by remaining open to receiving, even after the quest is ended, is important. Dreams will become sacred in context and meaning. Animal or spirit guides will appear to direct your attention to specific matters. The assimilation period afterward requires you to sift through the events that take place in the quest and in that process incorporate them into your being. There is the period of honing new skills, working with new insights, gifts, or powers. All this is necessary to learn to wield them properly. It can take many months, in some cases years, to accomplish, but it is always worth the effort, just as it is always your decision to accept the grace of Spirit in your life and undergo this magnificent transformation.

CHAPTER 10

UNDERSTANDING MEDICINE, MAGICK, AND GIFTS OF SPIRIT

There are powerful individuals who know the way to express the cycles and flows of energy passing through the Medicines and magick that are wielded by their knowledge and understanding. The pathways of Medicine and magick are found in the circles of life, in the cycles and spirals that are wheels within wheels keeping the paths of energy merging in and out of one another. These become the patterns of the Medicine Path; they are what the Medicine Woman watches for and has learned to weave in her work.

The Gifts of Spirit come to us in cycles as well and as we dance the spiral of life, they are timed to it. We are a part of these cycles. Each one of us is uniquely linked to life, and in that…magick exists. We can learn to tap into these forces and move with the flow to better our lives, heal, and grow. It is in understanding the cycles and forces that the Medicine Path begins to form under our feet, and enlightenment illuminates it for us. Just as there are wheels within wheels, there are also worlds within worlds—dimensions that are as sheer as veils. If we know the way, if we can see the path before us, we can slip between the crack in the universe and enter into them to know their mysteries and secrets.

We are a part of the cycles, wheels, and patterns. Look around yourself and you will see those you have long taken for granted. The cycles of the seasons reflect the many times we come full circle to begin a new stage of growth. The cycles of life itself are displayed through birth, death, and re-birth. Spiritual cycles exist as well, and when knowledge has been given, hidden, or perceived as lost it can once again be found. The shaman knows how to enter into the Silence and retrieve the lost wisdom. You can learn to do the same thing by understanding Medicine, magick, and Gifts of Spirit.

The Elemental Forces

The Element of Earth is seen in our own planet; its life glowing brightly in the universe radiates energy and links us to the cosmic forces. The Element of Water is a conductor of energy residing on the surface, in deep underground rivers, streams, and pools. Encasing the outer sphere and penetrating into the caverns and hollows is the Element of Air. We know that Air carries a wide variety of energies, allowing it to be transmitted to and from space as well as around the world. From the bowels of our planet's molten core to the eruptions of volcanic lava, the Element of Fire sends its energies throughout the world in a complex system of geothermal patterns. These Elements serve the greater whole of life. They reside in the physical world and we find them deep within our bodies. As above, so below; as without, so within; macrocosm and microcosm...all of life is linked, we are All Our Relations. The energies of the cosmic universe are unlimited, and when we learn to become the shamanic tree, to center between the worlds and Elements, we become one with Spirit.

The Elements are not restrained to simply the physical world, but reach into the Above World of the Sky People and Below World of the Ancestors. They reach through the veils and they hold sway over worlds of their own. Understanding the dimensions gives us another key to add to our collection and several other doors to open with it. These same elemental forces become our allies as we truly explore new frontiers. The upward spiral of life and the downward spiral of our ancestry allows us to witness the rising, falling, and linking of all life. Each life form reflects this spiral in its DNA, the building blocks that determine its genetic course.

As the patterns emerge they allow us to work with the flow of energy they hold. Going with that flow brings about harmony and proper actions. Fighting the flow brings accidents, obstacles, and roadblocks to the paths we walk. Learning to understand the flow and feeling it, each of us can ride the energy currents to our greatest advantages. Spirit knows our needs and provides for us when we remain in this flow, for they come to us as we can utilize them. When we confuse our needs with our wants, we begin to push our way through the flow, fighting its current and working against ourselves. Certainly we can strive for goals and achieve them along the way, but it is the journey itself that is important. Learn to listen to the sounds of life and hear the voices that will guide you. Learn to speak the many languages of the shaman and you will see this for yourself.

Energies of the Medicine Wheel

Grandfather Sun and Grandmother Moon rise to shed their light across the land. With their energy flows, their greatest balance is found during the Spring and Autumn equinoxes. You will find the Medicine Woman standing at a sacred site at these times, welcoming and working with that energy. She will enter into the Medicine Wheel to utilize its movements, and as it grows stronger she knows the way of sending her own energy to join in with it. As it weakens she can send away things that need to be banished from the lives of those served.

The Medicine Woman must be conscious of exactly what she is sending away from those whom she serves because her actions mingle with the universe and cause reactions. There is a mirroring or rebound effect and we must be prepared to face that as well. This awareness is a wonderful guide as to what we are or are not willing to do or accept for ourselves.

One thing that stands out in my mind about working within the Medicine Wheel is that you have a more direct link to the elemental forces. Those of other paths basically perceive these forces and entities as guardians that keep trouble at bay as they work, and as servants to carry out their desires. In shamanism it is a bit different. As the Medicine Wheel is drawn and the stones placed (or focused upon), you center with each one and integrate it into your work, linking directly with the respective spirit in each stone so the power is raised in a very potent way. This becomes intensified through the dancing and rhythms of the instruments as the trance state begins to take effect. It becomes a function of the whole.

Instead of accepting that outside forces are directing your work, the Medicine Wheel allows you to take on each of the elemental forces and work from the focal point of six elements and yourself as the seventh. You become one with them, and in that dance the cycle of power increases. It is an awesome experience every time. It is only a slight variation on what people of different cultural ways do, but the variation alone is significant because it takes in the patterns of life and the cycles as the shaman dances between the worlds. Clarity is amazing because you experience it on different levels of consciousness simultaneously.

The more experiences you have, the more symbolic these acts become. Spirit reveals great wisdom and insight to you on a very personal level, allowing it to expand. You see how you are linked to the universe, and though very small, you are not at all insignificant. The Medicine Wheel does have many layers or points of focus you can adapt to when you enter into it. It is more than simply a sacred space in which to work, and it becomes a school with many classrooms you can elect to choose from.

To dance the Wheel you need to have a purpose in mind. Learn to tap the source of energy that will bring forth enlightenment. Within the Wheel you are able to raise as much energy as is needed because you are going directly to its source. Group workings stir greater amounts through the uniting of wills and forming of a strong beacon or sending because the channel is larger. This can be matched by the individual who knows the methods of opening wide enough, one who has gained the skill and dexterity of maintaining that hold.

The energy of Spirit is a constant, and it is all permeating. So when you link with it, the results will come to you. You have to be willing to have your entire being "open for inspection" so that Spirit can mold you into the moment. No secrets exist at this time. You must give yourself as a gift then and there. A sort of "take me as I am and purify me to the core" will do. It will happen, and you will not have known such love or wisdom before. It is an intimate initiatory experience every time it takes place.

Medicine Teachers

This is the most important magick you can learn. In touching the face of Spirit, and those who serve as the Grandmothers and Grandfathers, the Medicine Woman holds the keys to unlock the doors of dimension. She knows that more of the Medicine and magick come to us from our Spirit Guides. Totems can be any type of animal to which you find a strong attraction; however, the issue is not your attraction to it but its attraction to, and selection of, you. They have methods of finding you, through magnetism, dreams, meditation, vision questing, journeys, or appearing in the wild in an unusual manner.

Spirit Guides act in a similar manner, teaching many things. The key to their magick is in becoming one so that you can see things through their eyes. A Cherokee Medicine Man once told me: "To follow the Medicine Path is open to everyone. To be the Medicine Person, however, means that you have an overriding obligation to help others in their path. The shaman doesn't cast a spell to speak with the birds, but takes the experience of being a bird and then talks to their brothers and sisters who are also birds." The shaman is then shapeshifting to journey or enter a state of trance and union with the animal.

In the process of following a Medicine Path one will be given Gifts of Spirit: songs, chants, dances, herbs for healing, items of power. The gifts are to be used not only for the person, but for those they serve in their community. While other paths may try to compel the spirits and elemental forces through the bending of them and the weaving of spells, the Medicine Person learns to be one with them, not draw lines of delineation or seek power in and of itself.

Understanding the Gifts of Spirit

Knowing what you need, it is for Spirit to decide what to bequeath as you open your heart to receive a transformational gift. When you enter the realm of Medicine unafraid, without doubts, and can show your true self, that is when you are gifted with blessings that help you grow. Today there are many who are seeking a quick fix, instant knowledge from a book, or answers instead of methods. These individuals will learn the hard way that it does not happen like that. There are many who pander to such impatience. My dear friend Tinker calls this "Candy Shamanism" or bluntly, "incompetence." Receiving the answer before the lesson serves nothing. It is the lesson that teaches us how to use the knowledge, and that must be earned, not just be presented as something to satisfy a sweet tooth. Taking the time to learn to do things properly, growing in the space of time that is right for you, and understanding the path you walk is so important.

Systems of magick can be learned, yet it is the true Medicine that is found in the touch of Spirit, and you honor it through your actions. This is the power so many speak of, and lest it be withdrawn until you see the error of your ways, you must indeed honor it. Spirit may be gracious and generous in allowing for mistakes to be made, but you cannot abuse that power and expect to maintain a proper path. To wield the forces of nature, know the intimacy of the Elements, commune with spirits—these are precious gifts. Gifts of clairaudience, clairvoyance, psychometry, prophecy, and so forth, are all meant to bring about peace, comfort, tolerance, cultural understanding, and a strong sense of balance to our lives. Receiving gifts and learning to work with them is a process of becoming part of this union. It is priceless, and should never be sold to the highest bidder. Be aware that with these gifts comes an increased responsibility and awareness.

The goal of our inner spirit is to make us aware of the cycles in life, to see the patterns so we can accomplish our purpose. When I was at Bear Butte, in the Black Hills of South Dakota, I was faced with an expanding horizon in all directions. It is the only line-of-site protrusion for miles. It was here my spirit was allowed to level out, and the landscape provided a canvas on which to envision greater things. Against the contour of the land, the sacred energies and honoring of the site provide a more spiritual outlook. I climbed the mountain and looked out realizing I was standing where many great spiritual leaders had come before me to listen to the voice of Spirit. I was looking at the world as they had. The wind carried the voice of Spirit to me and it confirmed the need to see all people as one, not lines of division but as spirits within bodies and a part of the whole. It spoke of the need to share our wisdoms and echoed the message I had been given so long ago...we need to be a bridge for others and honor All Our Relations.

The voice of Spirit can be found in the wind, upon the water, in the caverns of the earth, and the fires that burn in the home hearth. Learn to carry a Medicine Pouch with you wherever you go so you are always prepared to say thank you...it need not be very big, just large enough to hold some token gifts. Even in the most crowded places the voice of Spirit can be heard if you remember to listen, heed your own senses, and acknowledge your inner voice. Spirit moves in so many ways, and you can always ask for the signs to be a little bolder when you need that. The circumstances you are faced with will then have clarity and truth. See the cycles, see the patterns, see with the eyes of the Medicine Woman.

Variations in Gifts

Although our gifts and experiences do determine our lives to an extent, they also take away the weight of the responsibility through the sense of confidence they impart. We teach what we can to others. Sometimes we discover new ways of looking at things in the process of those teachings as those who come to us eagerly show what they need to understand. In this way we are exposed to new patterns of perception and become a student of the process. It is Spirit's method of getting us to look for the answers we know how to find. Sometimes this is done with rituals and ceremonies, sometimes with pointing a finger here or there towards a new door, and always it is by a responsible example.

What makes it all so interesting is that we can all share our abilities. The variations in them are what make us unique. We do not need to be jealous envying the gifts of others. What we need to learn is to hone and master our own, honoring them with our wielding. No one is greater or lesser than another, and we should never begin to fall into the trap of comparisons. The uniqueness we carry reflects the lessons we have learned, the vision we hold, and the path we walk. It is ours and we need to focus on that if we are to grow into our greatest potential.

The Gift of Growth

As you grow spiritually you will need to develop your own methods and practice them. Medicine is the magick of life. We call it Medicine because it is used to heal the mind, body, and spirit in ourselves and others. It is used to make us grow stronger, taller, wiser in our ways, and into Oneness with Spirit. It is far different from the tricks of the stage magician, and it is just as real as we are. There are other paths that speak of magick and power and offer them freely. You can find these same answers there too.

We need to understand what it is to be a spiritual person, to live a spiritual life. Spirituality is the primary focus of any Medicine Person before they learn to wield the magick, power, or create spellweavings. To receive our Medicine we must first become purified both consciously and unconsciously. The purification must take place whether by design or accident. Our spirits can cleanse us even when we are not aware that we need it. Do not be surprised when you go for a walk in nature or journey somewhere only to find you have been caught in a cleansing rain. Somehow

Spirit manages to create the situations you need when you need them. Sometimes you may be jolted into a shift of consciousness. It is at these times that the humor surfaces and you learn to laugh at yourself.

The Gifts of Sight and Sound

To be able to watch the flow of energy, reading its direction, and know its purpose will speak volumes. This allows you to be more alert to the subtle shifts and changes in your environment. The voices of the spirits are very subtle at first, and you almost want to brush them off as an over-active imagination, so be careful to listen and watch for them. Over time they grow stronger. When I awake I consciously greet the day thanking Spirit for the blessings that will come. Then I center between the Seven Sacred Directions and carry that center with me throughout the day. In the evening I repeat the process and in this way I am with Spirit around the clock. It only takes a few moments of my time. This is not some intricate pattern, it is not complicated and rigid, nor is it something that will interfere with any daily routine. It allows me to be alert to all the voices around me, and to recognize the triggers of my senses when Spirit wishes to touch me. If the need arises to shift my perceptions deeper I stop what I am doing, center again, then pay attention to everything around me.

When I was visiting the Coastal Redwoods of California time seemed to slow amid the strength of the ancient life forces there. At first I was swept up with the majesty of the place, but gradually I saw it for what it was—a marvelous land temple with great sentience and wisdom. These Standing People watch the world go by and hold the history of their home. That knowledge is now able to be tapped when I need to let things fall into place. Like my friend Advent says: "Revelation in a pine cone...one of their greatest gifts is their ability to think of the past and put things into perspective, regardless of how long ago (or how recently) those things may have happened." He is so right, and when I see a pine cone today I smile and think of his wisdom...and theirs.

My journeys have served to show me the many faces of Spirit, finding it everywhere. It is a part of me. By simply looking out a window, closing my eyes, or taking a deep breath, I have created the link. Emotions are our triggers, rising up to serve as tools that help us focus and accomplish wonderful things. By learning to set them aside after the initial onset, or wielding them in your Medicine, they combine with the voices of nature. You just need to learn to tap into them.

Tap Walks

I am often drawn to forests in very powerful ways. For me there is a kinship, and I love following their paths on what I call "tap walks." A tap walk is a focused venture into nature—communicating, listening, and learning from a wide variety of life. I tap into the spirit of the forest, or the spirit of the land I am crossing. I tap into the Elements, the creatures I meet, and the plants that grow. They all have something to share. Familiarity with the forests and places I love allows me to use them in my meditations. To visualize the places I have been and go there in shamanic flight links me to their energy signatures, expediting my efforts.

I am blessed to have forests all around me and I use them frequently. Whether you are feeling attached to these, or to other settings in nature, there is more for you to learn through such visits yourself. These places all have a voice and it will speak to you if you can open and listen. You would be amazed at the wisdom at your disposal. Some people work with individual trees, rocks, meadows, bodies of water, or mountains. I have found many places where land temples exist, and they are marvelous power spots with portals that provide a passageway to Otherworlds. The depths that these locations can take you to are wondrous. Whatever setting our Medicine takes place in, it must be one that we honor and respect. When this is accomplished you will find you are often gifted by Spirit with great knowledge, tools of power, or any number of other blessings.

Passing on Your Gifts

There will be times you may feel as if you just know things and express them in conversation as if they were old hat, when the words spoken are not yours...not totally. At such times you have been touched by Spirit, and become a channel, or cycle of information being passed for others to receive. To be of service in this way may seem trivial to you, but the words you speak can change the life of another in profound ways. They receive the message as it was meant to be received and Spirit will smile.

The journey of life grows into a living energy of its own and the arrival is but another springboard for the spiral dance to continue. We are all born with a hunger that is never quite satisfied. It is the inner spirit that knows that quenching. You must allow that spirit to quicken and lead you to the fountain to drink. Sometimes all we need is a gentle touch while the lessen comes in a whisper. At other times it is a stronger nudge, or as

Tinker says, "getting hit with a spiritual two by four." It is your duty to pass the lessons on when they can serve another, and your obligation to exercise them in your daily life...remember to lead by example.

The Pitfalls of Possessing Shamanic Powers

The spiral is always in motion and attempting to possess this power will invite it to come back and bite you. You must learn to channel it to flow naturally through you. Turning the power into a tool is a significant achievement. The difference in perceptions of that tool creates character in us, and therein lays the danger and risk of self-destruction or narcissism that is the pitfall of many unwary travelers. You must always be aware that the honor of what you have received belongs to Spirit. If you take it unto yourself and lose your humbleness, you are open to self-destructive actions. When this happens, the individual begins to glorify the self. They start thinking they are greater than others and their actions reflect this.

Personal views can become warped and actions justified as being worthy regardless of the harm they may cause. Such individuals are blinded by their own light. It is important to maintain a sense of humor and realize you are being treated to a lesson by Coyote, the Great Trickster, who teaches a lesson by making fools out of us. Catching on quickly will save you a lot of grief. As my good friend, Tinker, says: "No matter how Spiritual we are or want to be, the fact of the matter is we have to function in the mundane world as well. That means interacting with those close to us in a manner that's fair to all." She makes a valid point here, and if we can yield our credits to Spirit we can also find that sense of balance to maintain itself.

The Harmony of Relationships

In order to maintain healthy relationships you have to tolerate the needs of others and respect them if you are to expect the same consideration. Trouble comes when the flow or harmony of relationships is disrupted and others feel neglected. Sacred time does arise and you need to be prepared for it. Sharing this with a partner is wonderful and many of us do. Others must make their way alone, but it does not have to cause upsets in relationships when we are honest and express our needs openly. It is often said that the battle of the spiritual warrior is always with the self. We all struggle to find our paths, what works for us, and what makes sense.

Finding Strength

It is common to become overwhelmed. The teetering between faith and doubt are present in the beginning and sometimes as we go along our way. It is a signal to take the time to think things through, to sort things out, and draw your own conclusions. Even if you are taken off your path for a time, it will call you back if you are meant to walk it.

A good sense of humor plays a big role in your success and perseverance, and Spirit has a great sense of humor. I have laughed and cried at events that take place. Humor is a wonderful key, and an important one. You have to be able to laugh at yourself or you lose something in the process. It does not have to be serious all the time. Spirit understands and wants you to be happy physically, mentally, and spiritually. Loving and reflecting the love of Spirit in all that you do does not hurt. If you focus on yourself, remembering that you are a part of the greater whole, you will not lose sight of the integrity of your path.

As my friend Lune says: "It is walking the inner world of self simultaneously with the outer world of others. As a shaman you strive to walk in balance with all creation. Focusing on the inner self to the exclusion of the outer is a lack of balance." It is also when we become out of balance that we fall and skin our spiritual knees and Coyote is found in the bushes laughing very hard. We need to learn to laugh, get back up, dust ourselves off, and begin again. As long as you are growing from the experience and doing it for the right reasons, it does not ever have to become fascination with the self. By keeping your focus on the Now of the moment you will find you are able to let Spirit guide you and maintain a balance. Your spiritual path is so much a part of who you are and Spirit wants you to be good to your loved ones and maintain healthy relationships. The key to this is balance.

The middle ground is found when you come to know Spirit on a personal level. Learning to center, to ground your negativity, and to be one with Spirit will show you the way. Like Tinker says: "I am not sure all the pieces ever fit; we are constantly handed new ones that we must find a way to assimilate or discard."

To not attempt to journey because you are afraid to fail is selling yourself short. To not wield the Medicine because you are afraid of your inability to control it is selling yourself short. To not use the magick because you are afraid of what others might think is selling yourself short.

We all fail from time to time. It is the practice, persistence, and determination that leads to success. Patience seems to be a lesson that many of us repeat; we can only fail if we give up and quit, and growth can only come when you persist in seeking it.

When the path you walk is successful, you will have the courage to say you have your proof. If you want to hear me say that I was once there and that it is only a test, well, I will be the first to say that. If you want me to say it only happens once I will not. I have been tested many times, and over the years it has become clear that there are pitfalls at each stage we come to face on our own. The sooner you recognize the pitfalls the better off you are. It is a cycle we all go through in facing our trials, and no one is exempt.

The quest is ever to struggle against the self, against the logical mind, to see the illusions in life and lift the veil that blinds us to spiritual reality. To the warriors that strive to always grow, success is learning to hone their skills and knowledge. The one that does it with impeccable actions, personal integrity, and consideration of the ultimate importance of being true to their own inner spirit comes to know that success. The Medicine Path is a spiritual pathway of cycles and patterns melding with those of life and becoming a part of Great Mystery. It compliments our health on all levels, from the cellular to the surface and beyond. To understand these things is to understand Medicine, magick, and gifts of Spirit.

PART 2

WIELDING THE
MEDICINE

Chapter 11

Introduction: Part 2

Blackwolf Jones is a psychologist, an author, and a Native American man who I admire for his perceptive insights and honest answers. His message is that of the Listening Stick and heartbeat of the Sacred Dream—both of which take the shaman into the Silence where Spirit lives He said: "I invite you to stop...and listen. I encourage you to attend...and to listen. I urge you to experience...and listen." I liked that invitation and would like to extend it to you now. Come, take my arm and we will enter my lodge together for the telling of the ways. You are welcome to sit with me in a place that is not a place for a time that is not a time. Here we will explore worlds within worlds. The lodge of this Medicine Woman is a sacred space, one that was created long ago. Honor it as I give you the Listening Stick that reminds you to stay silent while the words you hear are spoken so that you may ponder them and know their meaning. In this lodge you will come to understand the tools to guide you along your path. Please, take your place upon the soft robes that are spread for you. It is the time of sharing and the fire burns to light the night.

The path asks something of all of us and what it asks is that we apply ourselves. We must come to know how to go about creating our own sacred space, to dance the Medicine Wheel, to meet with our Guides and teachers, to enter through the doors to Otherworlds where the greatest lessons are taught. Listen well then, so you may know these things and walk your path with impeccable integrity, with the ability to see and hear many things that others choose to ignore.

That which is of Spirit is disguised, and we must each learn to see it for ourselves. We have to think with our hearts as much as our minds. We need to recognize the little nudges and tugs that our senses give us—those "gut feelings" that we tend to want to ignore. You must allow Spirit's voice to grow strong...you must learn to listen. The physical teacher gives you the skills and knowledge you need to find your way, but the rest is up to you. Once you are there the true teachers will come. When you know how to seek them, the spirit teachers will show themselves. They will appear in dreams, visions, and on your journeys to instruct you in the ways that are your medicine. They will appear in real time, in real life, and they will speak with you of many things. At first you may feel quite stunned to see these things materialize. With experience, however, you will learn to accept the proof of Spirit taking action in your life.

All manifestations begin in the realm of Spirit. It must take place there first if it is to emerge in the physical world. My lodge is a place of such teachings. Here you will learn how to tap into resources, meet with your teachers, and receive your gifts. It will require effort, patience, and persistence on your part. If you are determined to walk your path, to make it yours, to share it with Spirit, to serve with your wisdom, then you will succeed and will know its rewards. You will come to know Great Mystery and to tap the energies of the universe.

Words conjure, ostensibly painting pictures with colors, textures, depths, and images to which we can all relate. They have power. Know this truth. The pictures they draw can weave intentions and concepts like the loom of the Great Spider that weaves the paths of life. They are mystical, mysterious, and very seductive. They can elicit emotion and touch your senses in many ways. What they draw from you they also draw from Spirit, but that is only the beginning. Words explain your intentions and the intentions with which you work must be based on integrity. You must remember that tolerance for others is one of the signposts along the way. If you are looking for the Hollywood image, power, or some form of glorification, you will find the emptiness within you to grow and drive you from the Medicine Path. Unless you seek and come to know the enlightenment that is required, you cannot develop the integrity of right intent. Those that experience the truth of this are the ones who stay and learn to accomplish many wondrous things. They are the ones who become impeccable in their ways and know the dignity that their own right actions bring them.

The wind howls through the night and rattles our windows, arousing us from our slumber. It tells us to be grateful for our shelter and warmth within the walls of our protective barriers. Lightning flashes and rends the skies as thunder rolls across the land to echo and shake the very walls that stand trembling between us and the storm. Fire and ice, earth and air, these forces have gathered to combine and create a chaotic scene of sentience. There is no hiding the force of nature that swells and sounds its crescendo. Listen, do you hear its voice? What is it saying to you? Some of us will know fear, while others watch and listen as if mesmerized by a haunting Otherworldliness. For a few who can see, there is mystery, magick, and the unknown all rolled into one, and its voice is explosive.

The power contained in the basic elemental forces of nature is magnificent. Nowhere can we see such displays of raw energy that are both chaos and perfection. These same forces set our senses to keening as their voices call out with a promise to part the veils that separate the realms of dimension. These are not forces that are to be controlled by whim or fancy. They are mighty and fearsome in their capabilities. These same forces lend themselves to those who are worthy, knowing full well no mere human dares to hold sway over them. Do not let the gentle side of their nature fool you. It is the trap that tempts the unseasoned practitioner.

Come, see the faces of your creature-teachers and your Guardians, listen to what they have to say, and grow wiser in the process. Then take the keys I will offer to you and open the doors to other lodges that await along your path. Store the keys in the lodge you will create for yourself. The Medicine Path is not one of recruiting efforts. People come of their own free will and thus, at the very least, have an inkling that it has something to offer them. I cannot tell you the stories I have heard of those who have stepped onto it, off, and then back onto it again a number of times. If it is meant to be, the call will continue.

Miseducation is cured through the efforts of those who do write about it, who create sites on the Internet highway and chat rooms where those of like minds can gather. Others gather in private lodges and some are misguided, yes, but there are many more who are learning and setting their peers straight. The truth of the matter is that when we walk our paths confused or misguided, Spirit always finds a way of setting us straight so long as we are willing to receive that guidance. We begin to learn from each other when the teachings take place between us. Questions make us think on ways to properly answer them, or lead us to other roads of discovery.

We must each do our part to promote enlightenment, speak only truths, and share our knowledge. We must strive to continue to learn as we make our way on this earth-walk. The only way to lead another is by example—to walk our talk. I see the changes taking place as a very positive state and a giant step toward the future. We have a wide range of abilities, talents, likes, and dislikes as individuals. We all work according to our own needs. In this way we have a choice as to what we want to incorporate into our own philosophies and spirituality.

The magick is a part of Spirit, and thus it is a part of you as well. You are your own magickal wand, your own shamanic staff, your own source of power. The wielding and forming of the will combined with our intent is what brings your magick to life. Thought can direct it, words can direct it, but it always belongs to Spirit. We bend and channel the energy to heal, to do positive work for society, to strengthen our lives, and to give back to Mother Earth. Intent is everything. Medicine works. I have seen many things that do not find explanation in the physical laws of science. I know the energy exists and I know Spirit—you can too. Throughout the chapters that follow you will be given keys to open many doors. Accepting them will be up to you.

Those of us who have had shamanic experiences know with every cell of our beings that Spirit, Medicine, magick, and energy exist. We know that energy is information and through the tapping of it, that information will come to us. There are many paths out there to explore and choose from just as there are many approaches to the discovery of Spirit. The path of the Medicine Woman is just one of them. You are welcome in this lodge, and you are welcome to know Spirit for yourself. I have always taught others with a simple pattern of understanding the elemental forces, how they apply to the Medicine Wheel, and how that can be danced. Combined with the skills of meditation, imagery, and honing the senses, the individual becomes a tool fashioned in a highly unique way. The techniques, skills, and understanding that come with their applications form the keys to open the doors of mystery that have evaded them up to that point. Honor Spirit, the teachings you will be given, and the path you walk. Walk your talk and you will walk with integrity. Nothing more will be asked of you than you are willing to give. Nothing more will be received by you than you are willing to earn. Nothing more will be hidden from you than you are willing to see. Spirit loves each of us profoundly, giving us the right to choose, the right to grow, and the right to become enlightened.

CHAPTER 12

ELEMENTAL FOUNDATIONS

Let me help you see through the eyes of a Medicine Woman into other realms that coexist with ours. Step with me through the four sacred Elements—Air, Fire, Water, and Earth—and amid the three worlds—Below World, Above World, and Middle World—to know them as I do. These forces are sentient, possess the ability to transmit through their energies, and hold vast amounts of information. Come to know the power of the elemental forces of nature that weave themselves throughout our lives. They are worlds within worlds and having that are both physical and spiritual.

The Eastern Quadrant, Air, and the Eagle

Step with me into the Eastern quarter of the Medicine Wheel so that we may begin a journey together. The Element of Air rules this quadrant to represent the breaking light of day calling out to scholars, philosophers, sages, mystics, and all those who seek wisdom of its Medicine. A highly refined objective behind inspired thoughts stimulates the mind and intellect to be creative. Being less subjugated to the confining gravitational forces of our planet, the Eastern quadrant is closest to Spirit. With freedom from emotion, it allows the mind all the space it needs to creatively process thoughts ranging from subtle to sublime.

In this realm, our consciousnesses first shift amid their own currents. This is communication of the highest order, when our minds become clear and our powers of concentration are heightened. It is higher learning and enlightenment. We can reach up to grasp what our minds hunger for from within a cosmic consciousness. Air's expansiveness allows the birth of ideas to be germinated seeds of the future. By understanding the nature of Air, we are able to work with it and realize that it can blow gently through our minds or tear through them like a whirlwind. We can hear its voice upon the Wind, speaking logically and pointedly as we tap the great receptors and transmitters of Spirit where no obstacle stands in its way.

Through this Element we begin to visualize our creations becoming steadfast and focused. We create and recreate ourselves, holding the image, imprinting it into our minds, and feeling it take root. This is the domain of pure thought, where chaos dwells at the edge of creation and spiritual form is born. Air itself is clear and allows us to see all the possibilities that exist, all the truths of creation, then put them to our greatest advantage. Our highest psychic senses are honed through this Element as it sets our minds free to explore and release them unencumbered by the physical restraints of the human body.

The inner spirit and consciousness find freedom from limiting emotions, allowing for a great deal to be accomplished. In the clarity of the Now, the journey begins to take form through practical, logical, and creative perceptions. There is room for humor and whimsy, but the work done will have a productive purpose. This Element is the cosmic college for the soul, and the classrooms are those of our own choosing.

Being the ruler of springtime, Air heralds an awakening in us, and it will do that as many times as it takes for us to consciously pay attention. We learn to become acquainted with our senses, realizing they speak to us of many things, showing us how to see into our own world and past the first veil of others. We learn to concentrate and utilize our inspired thoughts optimistically as we embark upon our path with flexibility. It flows freely to initiate change, clearing the clutter from chaos, and sweep open the way ahead leaving behind the turmoil of distraction and confusion.

Eagle is the Spirit Keeper of this domain, soaring to heights no other can reach, bringing us messages from Spirit, or taking our prayers on its wings to deliver them. Gliding along the thermals and alighting upon the firm ground, it is a creature of the two worlds that are closest to the Creator. Eagle soars high, dispelling our fears with clarity of mind as it reveals the unknown, connecting us to the universe. He helps us sense the changes in the world around us, in our lives, in the seasons, and in the will of Great Mystery.

Eagle speaks to us of rebirth, of light, of wisdom. He speaks of travel, healing, and instruction. The gifts of Eagle bind us to our responsibility, for the actions that result from our inspiration teaches us to think before we act and refuse the urges of yielding to impulse. We learn the unlimited capacities of the mind, of our wit, humor, and of wisdom, both given and received. He teaches the sacred taboos and summoning quest of Great Mystery so we may watch and become aware of its presence. Through this Spirit Keeper we are granted our first visions, know inspiration, and learn to decide for ourselves what is right. Eagle teaches our ethics, logic, and creativity that will serve as tools to fashion our paths so we may move forward.

The spiritual essence of Eagle is seen in its ability to transcend both the physical realm and that of Air so it is the messenger between you and the Creator. Facing the Eagle, you are tapping into the forces of enlightenment, the mind, creation, and messages. Eagle teaches clarity and the overview of the whole picture. Shapeshifting with this Spirit Keeper allows you to take everything in at once, see what is standing out, and then to focus in on it. It is like the soaring flight of the hunt that covers a wide range of ground before the prey is spotted, and then the spiraling descent to capture it.

Eagle is of the Air, the least emotional of all the Elements and thus its observation is not clouded by passions, emotion, or weaknesses of the more physical Elements. The eyes of Eagle teach you to focus on your prey or issues that need work, while the logical mind allows guidance in the perceptions of that work and how best to carry it out to your advantage. Air teaches us the arts of fantasy in imagination, fact in illumination and enlightenment, and form through the materialization of thought concepts. We learn the power in the choices we make, directing our lives and developing our philosophies. We learn the art of transformation through mental stimulation and the truths of the connections to the realms of Otherworlds. Air is the ruler of mountains, hills, and plateaus, which are home to Winds. Air has the ability to either calm or excite the winds. They can be tumultuous or docile, changing strides in a heartbeat as it conducts the flow of energy through the world. This is a powerful unpredictable force as it moves unhindered past stationary objects to glide around, through, or over them.

Demonstrating the forward and upward spiral dance of life or the downward flow of knowledge through inspiration, its invisible powers exemplify the unseen forces of the universe. Air presents us with dimensions that are realms within realms and the veils of Otherworlds yet to be parted, the entities that inhabit them, and its promise of more. Take a deep breath of Air and let it cleanse your mind. Exhale slowly and feel the misconceptions of a lifetime leave you.

The Southern Quadrant, Fire, and the Mouse

Step now into the Element of Fire found in the Southern quadrant. Here we have the eternal light, life-giving and shining from within, linking us to the universe and Spirit. This light is represented by the height of the noonday sun illuminating our paths so we may find our way easily. Fire is the essence of our being reflected in the light of the body's energy fields. It represents evolution through its powers of purification. Its energy is quick and filled with action as it swiftly changes to kindle the Divine within each of us.

Fire is the innocence we are born with and the trust we come to know through its protective powers while teaching the lessons of youth. The Phoenix that rises from the ashes to be reborn symbolizes the rebirth of our choosing, demonstrating the destruction and creation that allow us to reshape our lives while clearing a new path. In its physical form it must consume, feeding itself to exist and shifting shape to become transformed. It has the ability to purify and recreate all that it touches.

Fire rules Summer as the heat and nourishment of the growing season, touching our lives and urging us to explore. We become changed by those experiences as it shows us both boon and bane. We will see our way or become blinded by its light. In a dichotomy of give-and-take, the Element tinders its way with the power to destroy and annihilate all pre-existing conditions. It leaves a smoldering reminder of its volatile forces of destructive, purifying, and regenerative capabilities.

Though we may long to be near Fire, easily becoming mesmerized by its charm, its heat is scorching and will force us to step away. Its potency affects us physically, spiritually, and psychically as it takes action with un-bridled strength to create a certain faith within us. It tells us we are not alone, that Spirit burns within us as it burns within all of life. It provides the energy we need to take control of our action, focusing our wills, hearts, and passionate desires.

Fire is purity in a state of innocence, the incipience of all we feel emotionally, sexually, passionately, and spiritually. It represents the pow-erful potency of psychic energy, initiations, and communion with Spirit. It reflects the source of our personal power through our inner spirit, showing us the courage we need to be able to act and speak our truths. It can dispel illusion, reflect life back upon us, and make us face our fears. It initiates all aspects of our lives and transforms weaknesses, insecurities, and frustra-tions into strengths, confidences, and resolutions. In this way it protects us from ourselves.

Setting trials for us by presenting the character-building experiences we need to grow, the pain it brings must often be felt before we can learn what it is to be humble. Fire will teach us to feel compassion for others, to be empathetic, or through the error of hastiness to know humility. It is the heat through which perceptions are granted burning them into our minds and hearts so we will not forget. Through Fire's trust and innocence we learn to perceive the world around us, gaining the faith necessary to tread our path.

Fire is represented by the Spirit Keeper of Mouse that sees life through a microscopic view. At ground-level perspectives, that vision is focused upon what is immediate to its survival. By paying attention to details, it knows that the little things in life build to larger ones. In teaching the power of the will and the courage to back it up, Mouse demonstrates the need to be aware of everything, especially its vulnerability. Despite the constant dangers faced, the countless predators, and its size, Mouse main-tains an innocence and trust in its own senses to warn of risks as they arise. In this way it goes about its business trusting instinct to keep it alive. This is not a foolish blind trust, but one of a creature that has learned life and Spirit will provide.

Mouse is clever. It has highly developed senses, finds creative ways of escaping its vulnerability, and teaches the art of elusive movement. Know-ing the innocence of joy in all that is new through an insatiable curiosity, it sometimes jumps up taking a quick look past its limited horizon. Always coming back to a fundamental ground level, it proceeds to work from there. In that jump Mouse has gained a little more perspective, having just a glimpse at a much bigger picture. Mouse teaches us to accept the glimpses, enjoy the drama, and understand that growth feeds on faith. It shows us how to focus on ourselves before focusing on others, to find out who we are and where we stand. Through its innocent and playful passions, its faith in itself, and the purity of its heart, Mouse shows us the way through the dangers of life.

Fire has the power of truth, perception, and wisdom symbolized by Coyote. The Great Trickster will go out of his way to distract us from teaching the lesson that we should have remained focused on in the first place. He will apply humor to his antics, teaching us many things. As the cosmic clown, he runs in circles until we see him before he falls into a hole. We may get a big belly laugh and tears in our eyes at the foolish predicaments he elects to put himself in time and again. It is through his antics we come to realize that he must fight his way out of them, and in the end the joke is on him...or is it on us? It is the lesson hidden in his folly that we must learn to uncover.

Through Coyote we learn to laugh at ourselves and not take life so seriously. We learn that Fire can burn if we are not careful, and the need to always tend its presence in our nature to avoid our passions and fears from burning out of control. We learn how to shed light on our shadow natures, confronting them in purity of innocence. This way we transform them into positive attributes and evolve. Coyote knows these things and urges us to undergo trials-by-Fire to learn. If we are caught in his trap, the lesson is learned quickly or repeated until it is. He teaches the dichotomy of Fire, its fickle nature that causes fear, consumes, and the back-drafts that can catch us if we are not careful. Here we learn those backfires are spontaneous to leave us once burned, twice shy.

Another entity that represents Fire is the Dragon. Dragons are creatures of mystery, spoken of in myth, and have the ability to breathe Fire or enter all Elements. They can fly through the Air, they lair in deep mountain caverns, or dwell in the depths of pools, lakes, and rivers. Dragon represents evolution on a spiritual level and it is a conundrum, for just as it can bestow favors, so it can destroy or take them back. From the heart of the flames arise the Firedrakes; their yellow eyes ablaze and haunting, these Fire Dragons arch their necks with great dignity. They are courageous and willing to take risks. Being easily excited, they will crusade against evil in all its forms.

Respect, understanding, and a pure desire lead us to trust in our own abilities. Fire heightens our senses, makes us feel alive, lets us know when we are taking things for granted or being foolish. As the double-edged flaming sword, we will be burned if we attempt to abuse its power. Just as it tears us down, it builds us back up again to start all over in the rebirth of youthful transformation as our benefactor. It teaches us to learn to trust in the circumstances we are faced with, knowing Spirit will move us along our paths. Our senses are reborn within this Element as it encourages us to see life, recognize the love in our hearts, and explodes our experiences with a passionate will. Here we learn about relationships in the physical world and that of Spirit. Inhale deeply and let the Element of Fire penetrate your body. As you exhale, let the negative shadows pass away.

The Western Quadrant, Water, and the Bear

Step with me into the Western quarter of Water. This is the Element of receptivity, inner reflection, emotion, and intuition. Water reflects the twilight of evening, the rising of Grandmother Moon, and marks the transformation of day to night. Through its exploration we understand pleasure and pain, joy and sorrow, learn to face our truths and cope with the realities of life. Reactions to the lessons learned here are in a constant state of flux. Like the river that flows and winds its way through life, we can choose to go with that flow or struggle to hold it back and be overcome by it hindering the changes within us.

Emotions rise and fall like the waves on the sea, merging in and out of each other, then crashing to shore. Judging emotions and keeping them in check is the challenge presented here. In the process, we learn tolerance for those who are struggling with these lessons; we accept that they may be still learning, or perhaps have learned more than we have. Here we see the paths that others have chosen for themselves, realizing we have our own to walk. In that process tolerance emerges and we learn to nurture.

When we listen to our inner voice, we link to our subconscious, free our inner spirit, and embrace the cosmic energy of the universe. Everyone listens now and then, but truly hearing that voice (which is frequently in conflict with our logical minds) is not an easy accomplishment. Water is the voice of intuition examined to the depths of our being to know its truths. It helps us to discover the lies we are being told and the truths that we hear. Learning to trust our intuition when it proves itself repeatedly is the path that Water takes us along.

The inner voice is the counsel, the alarm clock of instinct, setting in motion all the warning signals so we can react. Physical sensations alert us as hairs stand on the back of our necks, queasy feelings appear in our stomachs, or invisible lumps appear mysteriously in our throats to silence us as we are about to speak. A profusely beating heart, sweaty palms, itchy feet, and clumsy actions will warn us too. Taking heed is important, and we must ask ourselves how many times we have ignored these things altogether...what happened when we did?

The Element lulls us into a slumber where our spirit communicates through the Dream Lodge. Drawing clear pictures we will understand, bringing vivid dreams that stay with us long after that slumber has passed, we come to experience the flux of our psychic abilities. They create triggers set off by the energy currents around us. Through them we learn to go with the flow, reading ourselves and the rest of life, be it in the physical realm or that of Spirit.

Through introspection we examine emotional feelings to understand why we love and how we should be embracing our lives. We learn to nourish and give love freely to others. That love is channeled from the bottomless well the universe has provided for us. Through this giving, we cleanse wounds, heal, and forgive in empathy as we have been forgiven. Our actions become redemptive, bringing hope of what can be accomplished. The same actions urge the completion of those accomplishments so we may harvest the rewards.

The healing qualities of Water teach that we must first heal ourselves before we can heal others. The tears we shed, the emotional cleansing they provide, and the release of pent-up feelings must be spent. When we are out of balance we undergo emotional storms, and when we bring things back into harmony the waters of the raging sea are calmed in the physical as well as spiritual sense. We are purified, sanctified, and baptized into our own initiations as a result.

This Element initiates the rites of passage, enlightening our emotional conclusions. To become a more desirable part of humanity we find the ability to transform ourselves through rebirth of the self. Thus we consecrate, cleanse, and baptize our spirits to be born anew into the light of the world. Water is the Element of our subconscious, guiding us through vision quests, shamanic journeys, dreams, trances, meditations, and deep psychic workings. These experiences help us glean knowledge through the benefits they offer.

Bear is the Spirit Keeper of the West. She allows us to see that the darkness of the night is the womb of Mother Earth. It is in the Silence that we learn to hibernate in our own inner caves, taking time to be introspective so we may discover that Water marks change, darkness, and is home to our deepest feelings. Its reflective qualities are the great smoking mirrors that force us to see who and what we are (or are becoming) as well as the death of our illusions. The cave of Bear is where our shadows reside, where we stuff and hide our fears, and where we go to calm the internal clatter that keeps us from recognizing these things for what they are.

Bear takes us to the place where we undergo our rites of passage. The love of life, playfulness, nurturing, and curiosity of this Spirit Keeper reflect and drive us to seek the truth in introspection to discover our answers. Bear teaches us to know the Dream Lodge, take counsel with the spirits, and receive their teachings. The Western quadrant is home to the vision quest and deep shamanic journeys. It is on this path to the West that the Element of Water guides us as we begin our walk and the service we are asked to give. Like Bear arising from hibernation, we come forth from that quest with a new perspective of ourselves and our calling.

In times when the spiritual strength of Bear is needed, it will be accompanied by the courage to support it. It is Bear who stares calmly into the rushing river seeking the answer to the hunger that gnaws from within itself. It is also Bear that sweeps into those waters with its powerful paw and gently retrieves the answer. She uses this same gentle strength to protect loved ones, nurture, and to survive in the world, enjoying the harvest of her labors before the hibernation returns. The cycle of Bear teaches us much about the Element of Water and the changes it can bring to our lives.

Water rules the season of Autumn with its long afternoon shadows beckoning us to reflect on the day that is closing. Our efforts lead us to the harvest by learning through attunement with its energies to understand compassion, tenderness, and receptivity. Here we learn to release all holdings going with the ease of motion to enhance our potential for creativity. The fertility and nourishment of Water is shown through the principle of love in a spiritual consciousness and vitality that is refreshing.

Water is the magickal element of internal shapeshifting where that which is seen as the ice of Winter melts into the swift flowing rivers of Spring and back again. It is the place of dreams that often come preceded by a mist, fog, or storm as sacred symbols of Spirit. It reminds us to be patient during the frozen times in the Winters of our lives for surely Spring will follow. Breathe deeply of this Element and exhale the negative energies and confusion within you.

The Northern Quadrant, Earth, and the Buffalo

Step into the Northern quarter and the Element of Earth. Feel her density as she draws you into her embrace, sinking into the soft fertile soil. This is the womb of the Great Mother, showing us the darkest hour of midnight. From here we witness the manifestations of life, the force of creation, change, and outcome. Earth's essence permeates, its energies are continuously interweaving amid all that is solid and formed. It protects our physical bodies and our realities gifting us with plenitude, solitude, and sustenance. It is here the material realm manifests, giving birth to function and form.

Through its gravity we learn to center ourselves, to "ground," to experience the cycles of life, death, and rebirth. We come to the wisdom of the past, the enlightenment of the present, and the possibility of the future, for it is the Element of reality and truth. Wisdom gained here is practical and applies to all aspects of our lives as we recognize ourselves taking on our respective forms. We can then lend that form to our creations, desires, goals, and successes. Discovering we can stand on our own, succeed, and receive the gifts of those efforts, we are humbled through our mistakes, forgiven for our transgressions, and see the errors of our ways. We learn to laugh with tears in our eyes at the simplicity of life and what we have made of it. The lesson comes home that if we fail to honor the values we were taught early on in our lives, we only create obstacles for ourselves and stumble along our paths. This is the realm of spiritual awareness becoming solidified through the explorations of the past.

Earth teaches that pushing forward requires purpose, that we must give tough love as well as tenderness, to keep our eyes and ears open, and know the gentleness of biding our time. Mother Earth's wisdom is that of maturity, old age, and of the Grandmothers and Grandfathers that have gone before us. She shows us how to make our way, do what is necessary to accomplish our tasks, and to avoid procrastination or suffer the consequences. We learn to relax and enjoy ourselves when we are through and want to reflect on our accomplishments. She teaches that we must foster moderation in all things because greed for the treasures of Earth will cause us to lose them. The traps are the temptations those treasures bring and our ability to retain our integrity when we have them.

Earth teaches us the value of respectably earning our luxuries and that we must be patient until we do. We earn these rewards in life through the process of structure. It's found in our environments, families, societies, and spiritual paths as we come to see the importance of each action we take. The evolutionary force of life unfolds through the transformation of the outward form of matter as we learn to apply our life's wisdom and act with the integrity of our hearts in the process. The treasures of the earth begin to present themselves. The culmination of our efforts shows in the results as processes are completed allowing the harvest of just rewards. Heart is at the core, and a major lesson to be learned is that of sharing with others willingly. If we become selfish we find that enlightenment will strike fast (like the sudden quaking of the ground beneath our feet). That strike helps us to recognize the realities we face, to see the fragility of life, the value of relationships—or to lose that which is most precious to us as a direct result of those selfish acts.

Mother Earth's enlightenment keeps us alert. It can be very slow to manifest, forcing us to keep plodding as we build our path little by little. It teaches the tedious lesson of practice leading to perfection, patience leading to achievement, and the value of applied repetition. Earth provides our food, clothing, and shelter as well as our medicines, wealth, structure, and virtually all other physical needs. The laws of this Element are those of our daily lives, of survival, and all too often we fall into the trap of taking them for granted. When this happens the nurturing becomes strictly physical while the spiritual aspects are lost to us. The focus of intent all too often develops into one of rank and file when it should be on heeding the lessons of change.

Earth is the place where the foundations of religion are built, but the stones of those foundations are found in Spirit and only hewn by humanity. Here we come to see that religion is of and for people while spirituality is of Spirit for humanity. It is the realm of discovery and formation of ceremonies, rituals, and mystical runes, along with symbols that represent the knowledge buried deep within its hidden caverns.

The Element of Earth teaches that death is a process of transformation. This lesson is sometimes painful, for we fear the unremembered or the unknown and think of it as a negative experience. Fear vanishes when we can see the rejuvenation and reincarnation of our path in future evolution. On the material hand we have the end of situations, conditions, projects, and struggles. We learn to empty our cups of unneeded habits, burdens, or concepts so they can be filled with new bounty coming our way. In the physical sense it is the ending of relationships, a way of living, or one consciousness for the next. Spiritually it is the beginning of transformation through freedom to a new life. When rebirth is understood and accepted, the movement forward is more positive. It is focused on making the most of each day, and on doing what must be done in the time we have to do it.

Earth makes magick come to life because it gives it form, truth, and wisdom, allowing the magick to materialize. In this realm the dreamer becomes the dream. In its physical form, Earth is the densest of the Elements and rules our sense of touch. We utilize that sensation in many ways, to heal, to form, and to sustain. We touch its face as it upholds our paths so we can make our way.

The energies of the Earth are exemplified in the essence of the Buffalo, the Spirit Keeper of the North. Teaching through great strength and providing knowledge, which instills in us the ability to give willingly of ourselves to sustain others, he asks nothing in return except to be honored. He does not want to be taken for granted, desiring only to be respected and to live in peace. He teaches that we are all parts of the whole, that our needs are all the same, and that we must find the courage to do what needs to be done. Buffalo asks nothing in return except to be honored, respected, to live in peace, and share the wisdom that we are all one. To the Lakota it was White Buffalo Calf Woman that gave the Sacred Pipe to the people. She taught its use in prayer, for it was both receptive of tobacco and giving of the smoke that carried those prayers while revealing the Otherworld of Spirit. Its bowl was fashioned from the red stone that held the blood of the people as well as the buffalo that roamed there. He shows us that to receive the rewards of our actions we must understand his truths, perceive the laws of life, and achieve success as well as sanctuary.

Buffalo teaches you to see sustenance, the foundation of life, that which provides for all your needs, and the inner wisdom with which that is done. Here you can examine all of life's lessons, the cycles of life, death, and rebirth as the circle begins to run its course again. It is the place of transitions and cold hard facts that must be faced. Through Buffalo you will learn that this is the Winter of the Wheel, the realm where plans for the future are made and the wisdom to compose them exists. Buffalo sustains your physical, mental, and spiritual life. Through those teachings you will learn that the Earth provides you with your guidance along your path, the right way of doing things, and that they must be done without procrastination. Here you will be shown the ways of wisdom are earned throughout your journey in life.

Buffalo teaches that our prayers must come from the heart and speak of our abundance as well as the gratitude we need to embrace for receiving our blessings. In this comes the recognition of All Our Relations. Through this recognition, honor them as sacred. All life forms must be acknowledged, exuding value through peace and tolerance, so we may come to our wisdom in our own time. We may not always approve of what others do; we may cringe, feel unhappy, or pierced with spears of pain. It is still not for us to judge, nor is it for us to dictate, because each of us must experience our own path our way. At such times we need to turn to prayer to seek understanding, ask to be enlightened, and receive the ability to accept what we cannot change with the strength to turn and go our own way. Nothing is ours through our efforts alone; we must realize that it is by the grace of Spirit that it has come to us. Inhale the essence of Earth and exhale the negative confusion of the paths.

We have now come full circle, realizing that the realms of the elemental forces exist physically and spiritually. Learning to center ourselves amid them is the path of the shaman who brings them into harmony. By mastering their lessons and maintaining balance, they may be walked in unison. Thus there is an awareness of what each of these Elements represent and symbology to trigger that recollection.

The real magick comes in the simple honoring of the Elements, the Sacred Hoop of Life, and the Creator. It is a humble knowledge that it takes all of us to create the whole—that alone we are only complicating things, and together we create the foundation we can all stand upon. We learn that the simplicity of universal truths for true magick is simple. The root of the word is "mage," which means "wise," thus magick is simply wisdom. It appears to be magickal because those who see it in action do not understand, and it is an unknown to the untrained observers. The knowledge of how to do something clarifies matters. It brings knowledge that leads to wisdom, and the wisdom teaches us that the truth lies within...we are the magick.

The Shamanic Tree

It does not end here however, for there are three worlds—the Below World, the Above World, and the Middle World—that complete the Seven

Sacred Directions. These worlds can be represented by the shamanic tree. The tree stands tall in the center, reaching its roots into the Below World of the Ancestors where the Ancient Ones step forth to greet us. They are those of elder ages who are wise and willing to share with us their knowledge. This wisdom contains ancestral memory, histories, and secrets of the past. It is a realm where the past takes form within the Now through what my friend Nofi calls "old memory." It is where we go to tap the resources of the ages, seeking wisdoms of the physical world that have been hidden.

Some will tell you there are dangers in the Below World. I say it is truly based on your intent and thoughts because mind, body, and spirit all work as one when you have purified yourself and centered. The higher your standards of integrity, the purer your intentions become, and the more impeccable your actions are the better your results in these journeys will be. One feeds the other to sustain you and raise your consciousness or state of enlightenment to a level of readiness.

The branches of the shamanic tree stretch their arms into the cosmos, to the Above World of the Sky People. This is the domain of Grandmother Moon and the stars, and Grandfather Sun and the planets, where the universe is seen to be alive with cosmic energies and populations of entities. It is the domain of the spirits that serve Great Mystery, and people from the Dog Star, Sirrus, which many believe we came from. It is here that our Guides, Teachers, Angels, and other spiritual entities or beings of Otherworlds gather to serve.

There is a great deal of energy from this realm that can be tapped. Grandmother Moon has a strong effect on our planet and us as she controls the tides in the oceans and our bodies (including our emotions and psychic abilities). Grandfather Sun provides heat and nourishment, the light of day by which we see, and the warmth that allows us to live among All Our Relations. These two alone are powerful influences, but there is a whole universe and more comprising the Above World. This is the home of Spirit, where amid chaos and confusion comes form and enlightenment. It is here the astral realms reside to mingle with the paranormal and timelessness that we are seeking to experience. It is the future taking form with the Now.

The trunk of the shamanic tree creates a place to balance the two in the Middle World of the Here and Now. This is the realm where spiritual and material existence combines as the shaman stands firmly amid the three worlds and the four Elements. It is here that wheels within wheels manifest, where the vertical and horizontal become enfolded within the sphere of Spirit.

Standing at the center of the Seven Sacred Directions is like being in the core of a gyroscope where the shaman becomes the true center of the universe. There is no differentiation made between what is physical and what is spiritual; they are blended together so life may be lived to its fullest. It is the Now of the moment. All that we have, are, and can be is present in that center, for it contains the essence of all we need. Bringing these worlds and elemental dimensions into the harmony of our lives is the ultimate goal of the Medicine Woman. Her work does not end here; this is only the beginning.

It is here you will learn to begin your dance of life upon the Medicine Wheel, see the cycles that spiral up and down the shamanic tree, and take your first steps beyond the world you presently know. You are armed with the tools necessary to begin the creation of your own pathway. Learn to walk your talk and honor it above all else.

CHAPTER 13

WORKING IN YOUR
SACRED SPACE

Sacred space is a place where time stops and you are able to create a safe, focused working environment and bring the Seven Sacred Directions together. It means separating from the rest of the world in a secluded location guided by your inner spirit to dwell in union with Great Mystery. This process is basic to everything the shaman does; in fact, the shaman tends to walk in this sacred space at all times. It is the act of centering and remaining centered. When you want to enter the Dream Lodge, meditate, journey, or vision quest, it is an integral part of the process.

The location you choose should be a private one. Outdoors it can be a secluded site atop a hill, in a park, by a lake, or even in your own yard. Indoors it should be a room where you will be undisturbed. Unplug the phone. Lock the door. Tell others not to disturb you. This is a time you will need to be alone to work. Most people still prefer the privacy of isolation, but necessity does not always allow for that. The size of the sacred space you are going to create need only be the diameter of your aura or about three feet, or larger if you prefer.

We will assume you have found your location and are ready to begin. Cleanse the area smudging it with sage, cedar, or sweetgrass, purifying it of any residual negative energies. Smudge yourself first, then the area around you, working in a clockwise direction and beginning in the East. Offer the smoke to the Seven Sacred Directions. Returning to the center of the circle, you may now use cornmeal to draw the boundary on the ground if you do not have a Medicine Wheel to work from. You can also use visualization. Some people prefer to place a stone at each of the quadrants and one in the center to represent the Creator, while others will draw the circle of the Medicine Wheel with a staff or their foot. This area defines your sacred space.

Elemental Unions

Next you will find a comfortable position either standing or seated. I tend to sit cross-legged with the palms of my hands facing up and resting on my knees. This allows the energy to enter my receptive hand (left) and cycle through me to exit from my projective hand (right) (if you are left-handed the pattern of the energy flow would be the opposite). Close your eyes and draw into yourself each of the four Elements while focusing on what they represent. Begin in the East with Air and follow in a clockwise pattern. Inhale the positive properties of the Element and exhale the negative ones. Deep breathing should allow you to follow your breath into your body and cleanse it with each Element. Each breath should take you deeper as you feel its cyclic flow throughout your body. After all four Elements have been invoked, you will focus on centering yourself between the Above, Below, and Middle Worlds in the same manner. Again the deep breathing should continue until you have brought each one within yourself. At this point you have reached true center and are balanced both vertically and horizontally.

The final balance is achieved by focusing on this center core within yourself and letting it radiate outward to extend to the perimeter of your sacred space. At this point you should be sensing a oneness with Spirit. It is here that you are safe, protected, and dwelling between the worlds. Initially the work that is done in your sacred space is that which will support more advanced intentions down the road. You will need to hone your senses, meditation skills, visualization skills, and understand the power of prayer.

Understanding that words have power is important. This statement is exemplified as we see that our own repetition of words penetrates into the levels of the subconscious where the old memories are stored, aiding to transform them into new positive structures. Certainly your beliefs become ingrained and are an intricate part of who you are. To give them up is to say a big part of you is wrong, so it makes sense that this would be something you must confront now and then as you grow.

This is not always simple and sometimes an affirmation needs to be repeated several times a day for a while. I was taught that it takes 21 repetitions to create a new habit or accept a new view. Repeating affirmations, chants, or mantras for 21 days will set the subconscious and conscious minds in balance. The purpose of the affirmation is to yield up your negative traits and replace them with positive ones. It is the power of words and positive thinking that will bring about the changes you desire.

Concept, passion, emotion, and wisdom are the essence of the elemental forces. The technique you develop to achieve change within yourself must be adapted to your own methods of working, but it is important to get the basics down first. Shamanically the transformations resulting from our efforts to evolve spiritually stem from shamanic skills and come from journeys. To journey into the old memories or beliefs and examine them is shamanic work. Prayer and meditation are two sides of the same coin. To pray is to speak when you need to communicate your thoughts, feelings, or questions to Spirit. It must come from the heart, not a few verses that have been learned by rote. It is far better to simply say what is on your mind and carry on a conversation as you would with a parent or trusted friend than to let empty words cross your tongue. So think about what you want to say and say it from your heart.

Meditation is listening to the voice of Spirit as it replies to you through that soft inner voice, or the visions that paint pictures worth thousands of words. This will come to you through the stillness and requires quieting your mind of idle chattering. This is what is meant by entering the Silence. Imaging takes you into the visualization skills you need and your senses keep you attuned to what is going on around you. In this way you are aware of your surroundings and alert to signals if you need to return to the mundane world for some reason.

Creating a Light Trance

You will want to begin with a light trance state at first. Like reading a book in a noisy lunchroom, if the plates crash to the floor you will look up, but if the din in the background remains constant you will know you are safe to remain engrossed in your reading. Deeper states of trance and journey work require your senses to be more focused, and they require your sacred space to be better protected from disruptions. So the senses need to be honed well.

Sounds can be separated going into meditation becoming isolated points of focus. Let's say the lunchroom is buzzing at its normal frequency and you have withdrawn from that. Your ears will tell you if you need to focus your attention back there. Meanwhile the book you are reading is talking about the sounds of a location and you can hear them. The author is discussing a setting while your mind draws from the words to create an audible experience. This same technique can be applied in meditation as you listen to the sounds of your environment and begin to isolate each one.

Let the example shift for a moment. Slip off to a quiet spot beneath a tree in the early evening where you have centered and created your sacred space. Hear the sound of the wind in the leaves, perhaps a squirrel in the upper branches, some songbirds calling to the setting sun, and the drone of insects. Each sound tells you something about your environment, and your ears become attuned to them. You can separate them if need be, focus your attention on any one specifically, or allow them to meld together and become a single voice. By allowing the sounds to meld, you focus on that voice. You can then set it aside to bring up another sense, and through this process, shift your perspective.

Now shift to the sense of smell. The scent of damp earth, fragrances on the wind, and the presence of an animal are detected. Perhaps the perfume of a wildflower growing close by you wafts in the air. You can shift again to the sense of taste and those odors will allow you to taste the nectar of a flower, or the honey some bees may be producing in the upper branches of the tree. Memory allows you to bring up these tastes as you focus on each one. Shifting again you can touch the textures of the environment. Recognize the touch of grass, the bark of the tree as you lean against it, the leaf that falls into your open hand, or the warmth of the wind as it passes through your hair.

Again, by shifting your awareness to that of feeling you can let the sensations of your emotions surface. You can draw upon your environment and feel it as a part of yourself. By feeling the coolness of the soil and its soothing comfort on a hot day, the song of a bird as it lifts your spirits, or the lull of the bee's drone as it calms you, the ability to hear many voices through this oneness becomes apparent. You can feel the caress of the wind's embrace and know that you are at peace here. The final shifting is one of vision. Even with your eyes closed in the meditative state, your senses have drawn together to create an image for you of all that they are perceiving. The textures, sounds, and feelings you draw from beneath the tree tell you where you are.

The Senses as Tools

You can see that your senses can take you to another place in time, creating sensual stimulation that brings to mind a clear picture with a sense of presence. The combinations formed from well-honed senses are important aspects of the visualization and imaging process. They are triggers to let you know if there is a change in your surroundings. Practicing these techniques and isolating them through the meditation process will let them speak to you. They will tell you when to go deeper into the meditation or when to stay near the surface. They become tools, so learn to use them well. Isolating, uniting, and trusting them is critical.

On a day-to-day basis most people take them for granted until the individual becomes impaired. If someone is disabled or handicapped they do not need to be left out of this process. They can work with the senses they do have. It is important to become conscious of them daily in all that you do so you can sharpen your awareness of them. It permits you to sense the subtle messages that Spirit gives, the shifts around you, and to know when the Elements are speaking. It is heightened awareness and it is a gift you can give to yourself.

At this point we will assume that you have created your sacred space, entered into a meditative state, alerted your senses, and left the mundane world to carry on beginning your visualization process. I will create a location for you through the power of words. The process of closing your eyes and allowing your senses to surface creates images in your mind through the energy of your surroundings. The process of meditation creates an arena in which you can use your own imagination, giving form to images.

Use Your Imagination

The root of *imagination* is *image*, and the ability to create images becomes a tool for the Dream Lodge, journey work, and vision questing as the shamanic experience expands. Children use their imaginations the majority of the time, creating worlds to play in and pleasant diversions. As they grow to maturity, that skill tends to atrophy from the innocent creation of exploration, because adults tend to lose sight of its old applications. When adults slip into a daydream, they remand their attention back to the task at hand, often feeling guilty for having been distracted. Worse yet, they may hear someone else say, "I have no imagination," "I am not creative," sewing negative seeds in a questioning mind. Everyone has this ability; it just has to be re-learned.

It is that child-like quality of being able to daydream that stimulates the imagination. This allows the individual to create landscapes that will take them into the next shift of the shamanic journey, Dream Lodge, or vision quest. While in the meditative trance state, you can allow yourself to daydream with focus. If you think about a tree it will appear. If you think about a calm lake surrounded by a forest it will appear. If you think about an open meadow, a mountaintop, or a cave deep within the hills, these things will appear. You just have to let it happen. That requires you to come back into contact with your inner child and be willing to play.

If the mind wanders, simply bring it back into focus. Like the senses, it must be trained. Once you do this a door opens and you are handed yet another key. You are not deluding yourself into thinking you have entered another dimension or realm, you know you are creating it, and that you are in control. It allows you to explore your creative abilities and form images...a skill that will become very important later.

By accepting imagination as part of your natural abilities, you have the arena to pursue a classroom of your own design. With such a paintbrush in hand you can create anything you wish. It is important to draw upon a place that is special initially, one that recalls fond memories, or perhaps made you feel at peace or in awe of the splendor of life itself. It does need to be a place where you feel safe and secure. In the meditative state, you are already well secured in your sacred space, but it needs form. This is where you put your imagination to work with all the colors of your mind.

Imagination Exercise

As an example of such a place, I suggest the image of a meadow near the edge of a forest. In this imaginary place you can walk near the tree line and see a deer trail leading inward. Following it into the dappled shadows of sunlight that spill to the ground spreading through the undergrowth, you see the roots of trees are bared along the path, and you must carefully step over them to make your way up an incline. The trail begins to veer left winding around the hill clockwise.

Forest creatures are skittering around in the branches of the trees. The air is warm, damp, and a refreshing breeze brushes your face. As you come to the back side of the hill you see a bush that has nearly overgrown the entrance to a cave. Your curiosity gets the better of you, so pushing back the branches you duck to enter and find the ceiling of the cave gives just enough clearance to stand upright. As your eyes adjust to the light you notice a faint flicker near the back and walk toward it.

The formation of a dimly lit tunnel off to your right calls you to explore deeper. The tunnel goes on for about 100 yards with a path of soft, damp sand. Fresh air is coming from the far end drawing your attention to a brighter light at the end of the tunnel. Your curiosity beckons you to quicken the pace. As you reach the end of the tunnel it opens into a cavern. Let your eyes explore the chamber where the walls glow from the myriad of crystals that are embedded in the rock. There is a fire trough in the center of the floor. Look up and explore all the nooks and crannies as you step into this secret chamber.

Shifting into Dimensions and Back Again

Letting your imagination take you from here, you can create anything you want. This has now become the center of your sacred space, a workroom from which you will begin to assemble all you need for furnishing the chamber. Take control. Do you want a work table, a desk, tools, books, chairs, or a smoke hole in the roof? There should be a source for each of the four Elements to manifest themselves. You are the creator of this space and can make it comfortable, secure, and as roomy as you like, coming and going as you please. It can be an escape from the mundane world, stress, worries, or the complications of life. It can also be a springboard for much more.

It may take several visits to get the chamber finished, but as your abilities and needs grow the cavern can and will accommodate them. When it has been visited several times it begins to take on a feeling of being at home and comfortable. At that point you can shift your consciousness to the next level. You may be ready to enter it through the Dream Lodge and find yourself going there automatically at night to work on your skills. You may feel you are ready to begin journey work and find a need to expand its capabilities. There will be no doubt in your mind when that time comes, and it is the next level you will explore.

When you are ready to journey there will be a need for a portal of some sort that you can pass through into other dimensional realms. The source of Air can lift you to the Element and carry you on explorations. The source of Fire and Water can take you to those realms, while the source of Earth can open a window, a door, or a passageway into that dimension. Perhaps you need an enormous tree that will allow you to climb up into its branches, or a thick vine with many tendrils that will support you as you make your way into the Above World. You can follow the tree or vine down into the Earth to enter into the Below World, working your way along its roots or into a hollow at the base. The trunk of the tree or vine is there to remind you that you are at the heart of the Middle World where the physical and the spiritual are one. Create the image you are comfortable with and work with it.

These new passageways will open into the dimensions where landscapes will await you and the explorations you wish to pursue. There will be encounters with strange and wonderful places, their inhabitants, Power Animals, Totems, Spirit Guides, and entities that will become your friends. Each encounter you experience will teach things about the dimension, but more importantly about yourself. When you enter such a dimensional realm it is important to be cautious and observe at first. You must learn the laws by which it functions, the cultural aspects and ethics of those who inhabit it, and never forget your manners. You are a guest in a strange land, in the abode of spiritual entities that did not necessarily ask you to come there, so you need to behave. Walk with respect as you present yourself to them. They will generally present a challenge to see your courage, intentions, integrity, and if your ways are impeccable.

Standing to these challenges means that you also have the right to expect the same from them. You should return the challenge respectfully by asking the name of the being you encounter and why they have chosen to appear. Ask what they have come to show you or teach you. It is always best to open communication with a proper introduction as to who you are, why you have come (this can be as simple as stating you want to learn about the realm), and what you are willing to give in exchange for the privilege of being there.

Trust your senses, as they will be raised to a new height to explore this strange environment. Let them bring back their messages so you can begin to understand things. On this level the subconscious mind is in control, functioning with its own expansive logic, and it can comprehend with acceptance things that the conscious mind would argue. What is fantastic becomes the norm and is assimilated quickly. You may find the ability to understand different languages, move with the speed of thought, receive telepathic communications, and any number of things.

You have now stepped outside your imagination to experience another reality. As you begin getting your bearings, note the landmarks in that area. Initial explorations are short, allowing you to become familiar with the surroundings and how things function. With each successive venture there is a gradual deepening to the probes, more entities reveal themselves, and you receive greater enlightenment. You are a visitor and cannot remain in these realms forever. Through your senses you will come to know when it is time to return to your sacred space.

Upon returning you need to close the portal that was used so that your own cavern remains secure. The close is achieved by reversing the process used to enter your sacred space. Withdrawal is then gentle as the senses and elemental energies flow with momentary focus. You let yourself sense the elemental energies slip away into Mother Earth. Step by step you return to a conscious state where you feel the solidity of your immediate environment return. Your senses are triggered by the choice you made and begin to attune to the new movement. Each sense, already honed, takes a unique focus and together they team up to act as a powerful tool. Our senses guide, warn, and protect us extremely well when in an altered state of consciousness. The trick here is in the level of trust we place in the senses and their accuracy. Time proves this to us.

It is necessary to shift back into the awareness for that level and put things in order. Gather yourself when you have finished, leaving through the tunnel which leads back to the cave entrance. Let your eyes adjust to the dimmer light and then the brighter light of day at the mouth of the cave. The Wind is gently rocking the branches of the bush that conceals the entrance. Smelling the density of the forest growth and the dampness of the soil, you now step back out into the dappled sunlight to follow the deer trail back to the meadow.

Songbirds are lending their voices to the setting sun, and the critters that scamper are beginning to settle in for the coming of twilight. Your senses are telling you it is time to shift again and close your mind's eye, to breathe deeply and draw back to your secluded space. Each breath takes you closer to the surface and the shift comes once again to let you know that your environment has changed.

You are back where it all began. Continue with a few more deep breaths, feeling invigorated. When you are ready, open your eyes. Settle into the physical reality, releasing the elemental forces and bidding them well. Remember to thank them for their help by leaving a token gift if you have not done so already. Break your sacred space by gathering up any things you may have elected to bring with you. It is advisable to do any journal work while your mind is still fresh. When this is complete the assimilation process begins and the need to focus on honing the lessons that have been received becomes important.

Once back to the mundane world there will be tests and the need to apply your new skills or knowledge. At that point you may experience a lull in your spiritual path. This is a time of restoring energy to the body, attending to family, work, and other matters. It leaves the open space needed to enter a new cycle of growth. The skills and knowledge you gain find many applications as you walk your spiritual path. Learn to use them to serve your own basic needs, but more importantly to serve the will of Spirit and All Our Relations. Learn the side trails that lead to dimensional sources of even greater growth. Utilizing your sacred space becomes second nature after a few of these journeys, which become tools of simplicity to be used in a wide variety of ways.

You may discover glimpses of the future are shown to nudge you onward. These are clues as to what lies ahead, whetting your curiosity, making you explore a little deeper, inspiring you to try a little harder, and giving you the confidence to do it. When you heed the call these visions stir within you there will be other discoveries along the way; blessings await as Gifts of Spirit that will make the journey a little easier to grow into your path.

Working with the Doors of the Medicine Wheel

To lift the veils of Otherworlds, to slip the boundaries of the mundane and know of realms that reside amid the dimensions, to step through the doors, this is to dance the Medicine Wheel. To explore it one must enter sacred space. To listen to the drum and feel its rhythm pounding in your heart or to become lost in the beats and pause between them is to enter into the realm of Spirit. Let the music of the drum course through your veins and lift your feet to dance. Come join me in the Medicine Wheel.

There are four main doors within this space that are portals to Otherworlds. Through them you can enter the domains of Air, Fire,

Water, and Earth. There are three worlds that exist here, the Above, Below, and Middle. Through them you can journey and quest beyond your wildest dreams. Exploring these worlds allows you to delve deeper into Otherworld realms of the elemental forces, realms of multiple dimensions to explore. The possibilities are endless for the serious student by recreating the Medicine Wheel again in the realm that has been entered.

Entering Dimensional Boundaries

When you step into a dimensional boundary, the world itself begins to go just slightly askew. The directions appear to shift slightly off their normal placements creating cross-quarters. Colors intensify, forms become more defined, sounds become sharper, senses go on alert status, and subtly you have entered into Oneness with Spirit. When you enter the spiritual realms of the individual quadrants, there is often a shimmer to the air itself or an ability to perceive the energy of that Element. The Medicine Wheel takes you into spiritual realms with great depth and interaction. It represents the realms of many worlds, those of plants, animals, minerals, colors, Totems, elemental forces, and the planets.

Through the teachings of my friends I was taught the methods of creating a center of balance within myself that was deeper than any I had previously known. They showed me a method of finding the Inner Wheel, which is our harmony with all of life that resides within us. It can be visualized to explore all aspects of the self. It can be a method of centering and drawing yourself into the elemental forces within each of us—then carrying that awareness with you throughout the day. Along with that is the visualization of an Outer Wheel. When you become centered in this way you are always within sacred space and always walking with Spirit. In the Medicine Wheel, the forces of nature and the Elements are taken on as aspects of yourself, and interaction with the entities takes place. As an example, when you enter to the East there is not only a summoning of the beings of that quarter, but entering also entails taking in the myth of the East knowing all that it stands for and all its associations. You become one with the quadrant. You merge with Eagle and dance with him. You meld with the Air and become part of a deeper union. You shapeshift and spiritually begin to manifest these traits within yourself. Then the next Element comes into play and the process repeats itself as the Wheel is drawn together in a spiritual dance.

In the center of the Wheel is the Creator stone representing Spirit in all its creative qualities and the center to which you ground. While working from the center of the Wheel, the link between the worlds is established. That is a lot of accomplishment in the construction of the Simple Wheel itself, so you can see where this can get quite intricate when working with a Ceremonial Wheel that is composed of 36 stones. I begin all my teachings with a basic Wheel of five stones. There is a lot of power summoned at this point and it is more than sufficient for the majority of work any beginner is going to attempt.

Working with a Simple Wheel

While many different Medicine Wheels can be put to use in your practices, it is important to understand what each stone represents and how to use it. Every stone is symbolic of a different aspect of the shamanic teachings. The Ceremonial Wheel contains the entire cosmology as each depicts a teaching of that cosmic knowledge. Taking five stones, one for each direction and a center stone to represent Spirit, you can make a physical layout (you can also use a Pocket Wheel or visualize the layout). Gathering the stones is a process that entails seeking those stones that call to you and ask to be a part of your pathwork. These stones must speak to you and tell you their placements.

To begin working, place your five stones in their appropriate positions. Smudge yourself and the sacred space around you. Take your position either standing or sitting and focus on centering. Know that when you face a direction you are summoning that direction to you, the direction to which your back faces is then evoked from you. To face the East is a position many are comfortable starting from. You are focusing on the Element of Air and Eagle. You are tapping into the forces of enlightenment, the mind, creation, and messages both to and from Spirit that the Eagle represents. From behind you the elemental force of Water is the perspective from which you are perceiving the quadrant of the East. In other words, it is the Bear and its ability to go within, to seek the Womb of the Earth Mother, to reflect through the Great Smoking Mirror of introspection as the work is done. It is the emotion of nurturing, loving, and being kind to the self that combines with the intelligent way the messages are received. It is this internalizing that helps you to understand that which you face.

The Road that runs from East to West will provide insight along the way, but it is not enough to teach you right from wrong, and it is the Good Red Road (North-South axis) that provides you with a course of action to follow. Through the center you can balance the two and walk in harmony using the lessons learned on both. This is the place where Spirit dwells within the worlds, within you, and beyond. It is the place of union from which you can encompass all perspectives by turning in the direction to which you are being called, nudged, or where you are focusing your will.

The Wheel of Enlightenment is an extension of the simple Wheel. From the center, the Roads are extended outward beyond the boundaries of the Wheel itself, and another, smaller circle is placed at the end. It is just large enough to stand or sit in comfortably. These satellite Wheels are then quartered, and you stand in each satellite for a specific purpose. There you meld completely with the Element itself and shapeshift with the Spirit Keeper so that you are perceiving through its eyes as you examine each of the cross-quarters. It allows you even greater perception as you look to each of the others while focusing on a specific objective and examining it in each aspect. The overview from there is tremendous.

To understand the meaning of the South, the West, and the North through the eyes of the Eagle in the East, and the logic of the spiritual mind or cosmic consciousness, is astounding. The process then continues in this way as you step into each satellite position. Once all four satellites are completed, another circle is drawn that encompasses it all. This is the Circle of the Universe. It allows you to walk the perimeter and see into all realms, to walk between them, and to mingle with the spirit entities that can help you. You walk there with Spirit, seeing through the perspective of the Creator's eyes and what I often express as looking through the eyes of Spirit to watch It looking back at you. An interesting concept, but once experienced, it is awesome.

The Wheel of Enlightenment, as I have come to call it, lends you the perspective to see further, teaching you to examine any given situation or question, and conclude with the best advice you can receive. There is nothing here that cannot be dealt with if your eyes are open. Through using this wheel you discover how to be objective, dissect, create, then to grow in awareness and enlightenment in any given circumstance.

The Ceremonial Wheel

To understand the importance of the Ceremonial Wheel you must understand what each stone stands for and its particular mythology. In the Ceremonial Wheel the various aspects of the Moons, Seasons, and Clans come into play. There is much history that is involved when you summon those powers, and extensive study is involved before you enter into the workings of such levels. In your leisure you can continue to study, but practice the two Wheels presented here in the meantime. They have served me well and I know they will do the same for you.

CHAPTER 14

SPECTRUMS OF SPIRITS

There is so much I want to share with you about the spirits that inhabit the dimensional realms. These beings are the essence of life as it exists there. Those unschooled in the Medicine Paths may find it difficult to conceive of this, but our Guides do vary in every conceivable way. Their differences range from the subtle to the dramatic. Though you may seek them out on your own, there will be those who seek you as well. They deserve to be treated with respect, and you can expect the same from them. Once contact is made and a relationship is established with any of the spirit world inhabitants, you are on your way. They will want to see effort on your part and rightly so.

I am highly skeptical of anyone, human or spirit, that comes to me offering something for nothing. There is always motivation behind an action, and if I did not request it, if Spirit did not send it my way, I want to know why it is offered. The trouble is these free gifts do not reveal themselves as having a catch until it is too late and you are standing knee deep in muck. As a rule, I decline these offers as graciously as possible, and I highly recommend that you do the same. Learn to trust your instincts when they tell you things, for their warnings will be clear enough. If the feelings you get are warm and embracing then move ahead. Always make sure you know what you are getting into before taking anything at face value. It is just common sense.

Totems

Remember that Totems are animals that have a kinship to an aspect of your own nature. When they appear, they speak in ways that are innate. You begin to sense their character traits, study them, and come to know them quite intimately. Therefore, you will find you can read their mannerisms knowing what it is they are trying to tell you. It is important to notice the direction they come from. It tells of the perspective they are taking as they try to express something. For instance, a Totem coming from the West would signify a need to be looking from deep within yourself and reflect upon the message they are giving you. It would be viewed from a standpoint of purification, healing, or examining your emotions.

Looking to the direction the spirit is headed will tell you what the issue being addressed is founded upon. A heading of South would indicate you need to look for an area that requires you to trust the innocence of the situation, or examine it because it has stirred your passion and sense of adventure. It could just as well require you to have a reality check or undergo a trial-by-Fire.

Totems always carry a message relative to their own nature, as well as to guide you to view something that you must understand or protect you in some fashion. They will allow you to shapeshift with them, merging for a greater understanding of the lessons they teach. They have the ability to speak with you on a telepathic level. Through all this the message tends to be about you, your life, or the lives of those you are touching. Generally it is about growth, or sometimes an inability to see things clearly. Or sometimes the message may draw your attention back to your spiritual path.

Power Animals

Power Animals are interpreted two ways, either as lead Totems or as separate entities all together. I see them as lead Totems that reflect the dominant trait in the personality of the individual. They may take turns with the other totem spirits, but they tend to dominate throughout your life. Animal Guides tend to come infrequently, perhaps even only once or twice; they are not as familiar to you and you may need to look them up to understand their particular message. These entities come from any classification of species in the natural world (be it extinct or not) or they come from other dimensional realms. They would have a very definite purpose and appear in a very unusual way to stand out so that you would take notice of them.

Spirits of Place

There are also the local spirits of a specific location, the Spirits of Place. These entities are those you must actively reach out for and contact with reverence and total honesty. They do not ask to be your friends, nor do they particularly want you to intrude on them, so you must be humble and go before them only with reason to do so. Along with all these beings are the entities that are of other dimensions who follow the rules or laws of the realms in which they dwell. Not all are pleasant or even willing to work with you and you must be on your best and most cautious behavior with them until you get to know them and earn their trust.

Recognizing Spirit's Presence

Spirit Guides tend to take on luminous shapes of light or human form as they come from a higher realm of cosmic consciousness. As teachers they sometimes stand at your side in the mundane world, allowing their presence to be sensed. You may hear them speak and even see them manifest. The number of spirits that work with an individual will vary widely, and you can have anywhere from one to several. Spirit Guides will often come in groups to put on a drama teaching ceremony or instruct in the methods that need mastering. Now and then they will bring a friend to observe or share.

There is a knowing that comes over you and you will recognize, or at the very least suspect, the presence of spirits in your work. Introduce yourself by your Medicine or spiritual name if you have one. It will be used in all future encounters as they are linked to a universal mind and word spreads faster than a wildfire, so you will become "known" to them. It is important to learn to be honest with yourself and with them. Sometimes doubt may set in when there is nothing to gauge an experience against other than what someone else has told you, and because of the reality check that the logical mind demands. It wants to fight you at every turn initially and will try to convince you that these encounters are imaginings. You have to experience things and be tested by Spirit so that you gain your confidence and learn to apply your abilities along the way...counter it with faith, and fear with courage.

Perhaps the entities will nudge you to turn on the television only to find a program that catches your eye pointing out an important issue. They may direct the same message three or four times in different ways if it has not gotten through. It could be an article in a newspaper or magazine, a conversation between strangers in a public place, or something said by a child clearly impressing you with its relevance. They have subtle voices, and you begin to develop a sense of humor about their methods.

People often ask me how to recognize signs and omens, and I tell them to pay attention to everything. When things start standing out we need to recognize their importance. Some individuals believe this to merely be coincidence...but I know better. There is a reason for everything. You have to look and listen with your heart...hear the whispers and see the shadows that move. It can come in the wild, in dreams, in visions, or just about anywhere your attention is focused. If you want an answer in a specific place you can focus your attention there and these beings will see that you receive it in that medium. Spirit uses every available venue to reach you at all times.

This does not mean that all day long you are being given critical signals of things. When you are troubled, struggling, feeling lost, or being warned, these messages will come. It is usually when you are best at blinding yourself to them. That is why it takes a conscious effort to be aware of what may appear to be quite coincidental. The rest of the time you will usually pick up on them quite naturally. You know when you are in the flow of life and the current is broken by something as it grabs your attention and speaks to you. Our Guides always send signs, and you will come to realize how many you have chosen to ignore. Hindsight is a beautiful teacher and the spirits seem to have some very challenging jobs. I often think of people who go through life ignoring the signs of their Guides and how frustrated those Guardians must be. It is up to each of us to be aware, become enlightened, and to listen to our Guides when they appear. Some never do, and I am pretty sure those spirits have to just be content with the roles of a Guardian.

Lucid Dreaming

In working with spirits, dreams become powerful tools. Today it is common to refer to this as lucid dreaming. It is a shift in awareness while in the dream state. If you are aware of dreaming and seeing through the eyes of your spirit, you are dwelling within the Self and taking an active role. You might practice searching for a tool, book, or a door and find these things just begin to appear in the dream. Later your dreams may show you where you can find these objects in the physical world. The dreams serve to expedite journeys and explorations. My Guides are always there in my lucid dreams, so if you are new to this begin looking for yours.

Start with simple techniques like seeing the backs of your hands or looking down at your feet. As you get better you begin moving things around, change locations, and even change events. Be it your own energy or that of the spirit teachers, things in the Dream Lodge are literally comprised of thoughtforms. The settings and entities you encounter appear just as solid and real as they would in the mundane world because you are equal in form there. It is a bit more fluid as the density is thinner and you can easily weave them to your liking, utilizing all your senses as tools just as you would in the mundane world.

This is truly a classroom, and you need to allow your teachers control. You should follow their instructions until you learn how things work there. You will learn more that way than if you were to interrupt the lesson and play around. Restructuring the dream you are in is a big temptation, but once you see that you can do it you tend not to do so. Your teachers will create a comfortable setting and gain your attention in the process. If you are dreaming and no teacher is present, the dream will then lend itself to being an arena to practice your skills and enjoy the fun of shifting things. For example, you may want to rearrange the furnishings of a room you have entered, or change the environment in some other way. You may want to alter events that are taking place. You discover that your thoughts are in control of what happens and your intentions direct the energy being used.

Teachers in Your Lucid Dreams

Before going to sleep you can often request a specific teacher, or issue be addressed, a certain setting be used, or ask for a continuation of a past session. Leave your teachers an open invitation to come and visit with you, setting the boundaries only on the types of entities you will receive. Patience is necessary, because you will not dream like this every night, but frequently enough to keep you quite busy. My idea of control is control over my own actions, not those of others, or those who may choose to teach me things. It is a dream journey, a bit different from those that stem from your meditative and imaging sessions, but just as valid. Your guides will speak to you when you learn to let them be themselves and observe their actions.

Guides come in dreams because they can transfer thoughts more readily. It is not uncommon to see animals acting and speaking aloud as a human might. Entering your Dream Lodge allows them to shapeshift into your world. The animals physical environs figure into their interpretations on a universal basis. Usually you will take a much deeper look into the significance of their traits when they become a Totem or Power Animal. The animals' characteristics and habitat combine to teach you their vulnerabilities and strengths in how they hunt, explore, discover, fight, defend, feed, and live.

Elemental forces will present themselves to you as well. Whether you train your senses to know them or not determines the level of communication you will have with these wonderful energies. Each Element relates to a direction, season, animal, mineral, and plant. The deeper we study this, the greater our capacity to know their voices. These forces can often relate to specific settings, and their sudden appearance will trigger that relationship in your mind. At that time it is always to apply the lesson you are recalling to the immediate situation in a creative way. If the Element is dry, wet, hot, or cold is a clue to its presence when you are being approached in or out of the Dream Lodge.

Remember by studying animals' traits you learn much more than just the universal interpretations of Lion representing courage, Bear introspection, Eagle a message from Spirit, or Crow telling you change is on the way. The environment not only dictates the lifestyle of the animal, but its dangers and ability to adapt to a given terrain or situation that speaks of its prowess. What the animal feeds on tells you what it seeks to gain as its predators demonstrate what is to be feared. Assimilating those traits in your journey through life will aid you in your evolution.

Spirit Keepers

The entities that dwell among the dimensions of Air, Fire, Water, and Earth demonstrate the ability to step into a quarter of the Medicine Wheel. Their abilities will hold greater meaning for you and prepare you for what will transpire next. It will also lend you the knowledge to select the proper quarter for the work you plan to do. In Chapter 12, we discussed the meaning of the Spirit Keepers of the four quarters. Now, you might be asking what it would mean if one of these Spirit Keepers is also one of your totems. Within the context of the Medicine Wheel they have specific roles, and those roles take priority. You may well have a greater understanding of a particular spirit essence and its nature, but here these spirits are Guardians of a realm, and their roles are even more defined.

They are elusive and some individuals never do see them. These entities are able to appear as attributes of their Elements as well and much of the symbolism of the four Elements is synonymous with their Spirit Keepers. Otherworld entities can manifest as apparitions or as mists that are anywhere from gray to colored. They can espouse human attributes, or come in the form of drifting or dancing lights. These lights have been called Earth Lights, phantom lights, and Will-O-the-Wisps. They range from silvery to neon white or shimmering colors. This is often in accordance to your nature of sensitivity.

Those spiritual entities that are presented here can interact with you across dimensional borders; however, there are many others that exist as well. You now have some fundamentals to begin your own dance as you learn the patterns within the Medicine Wheel. These beings will escort you through the Otherworlds and teach you many wondrous things so long as you keep an open mind and heart, heed your intentions, walk with integrity, and strive for impeccability in all your interactions with them. We are all spirits, all born of Spirit, present in all that exists, we are energy flowing in one form or another. May those you meet enlighten and inform you, may you see beyond the illusion of the physical realm, and may you know there is much more to life if you open your eyes to see.

CHAPTER 15

RECEIVING GIFTS
OF SPIRIT

When someone says they have been gifted by Spirit, what they are saying is that they have discovered and received permission from Spirit to use their talents, been blessed with teachings, or have been shown how to make the tools of power that will allow them to serve the Creator and All Our Relations. Sometimes these gifts are made known through your teachers and Guides, and sometimes they come from Spirit directly. This can include being given a song or dance to activate your gifts, or you may be shown a ritual or ceremony for their utilization, or given the use of plants for healing along with all the things that will serve to strengthen them.

You can be made aware of your gifts through a serious illness that causes you to come out of it stronger in some aspect of yourself. Sometimes it will happen after a severe accident causing you to have an out-of-body experience accompanied by a moment of great enlightenment. Occasionally these things will surface on their own at an early age or as you mature and have the time to recognize them for what they are. These experiences can be very strange. Sometime visions explain things in cryptic ways, or repeated dreams hint of a spiritual path and may include teachers.

This can vary from one time to the next and is cause for many to seek out the shaman to help with interpretations.

It is not all thunder and lightning, and just as often it is the subtle hand that plants a seedling within you to grow and manifest later. In this process there are many psychic talents that can manifest. These include looking into the eyes of another to read her spirit; knowing things about people by touching their possessions; the ability to see, sense, or feel auras; the ability to see spirits of those who have dropped their robes; or healing by touch. These gifts are useless or at best confusing unless you come to understand how to deal with them.

Seeking answers is part of the discovery process, and it is not uncommon for individuals to feel a bit odd about discussing these things openly at the initial onset. It is important to know that along with the gifts come the obligation to serve, the power to wield them, and the wisdom to know they are only tools. There is a wide range in the methods by which the gifts are received. Some are passed on genetically, by gender, or through ritual initiations such as a vision quest.

Areas of interest are often spiritual urgings or nudges to open your eyes as they call out from deep inside you. As intuitive skills manifest, you develop strengths in that area by understanding the language. Potent impressions urge you to say things to others that may or may not make sense to you personally. Simply following those nudges could unlock the door to other abilities just waiting below the surface, and your own Guides may begin to appear. It is then that you must choose to believe in yourself or brush these experiences away as a figment of the imagination.

By remaining open to receiving the silent counsel of Spirit in order to expedite your efforts, you are using a fundamental key. Many people have similarities in the gifts they possess and you will find some are able to shape dreams, work with weather, will things to happen, travel out-of-body, or some other talent that is either different from or similar to your own. Please remember if these gifts are not handled responsibly they can turn on you or be taken away. The same thing applies when talents are neglected. They wane and atrophy, taking much effort to bring back. If you work with them for the greater good of All Our Relations they have a tendency to grow as you gain more control and confidence. Trusting your intuition leads to greater discoveries, and many of your talents will manifest through self-teaching methods as you progress.

Winds may bring you messages or allow them to be sent. You may be able to read the clouds where the entities of the Air show their faces or create images. They do know how to capture our attention and will call to us indoors or draw us outdoors to look up at the sky. You may feel the change of seasons intuitively, storms may speak, or you may be able to call up rain, hills, trees, and animals. This is not something that is for everyone, nor is it done on a whim, but it is part of the path for many of us. These gifts should never be used for the sake of enjoyment, play, or boasting.

Each Element has its own essence and sentience and you may have an affinity for any or all of them. The entities that dwell within these realms sense our emotions and passions acting upon those sensations. The Element absorbs our intentions and events take place. The hidden dangers and consequences to our actions are always the next phase to be dealt to us. Be prepared for that. Know that you are responsible for your acts and that carelessness will bite hard when it returns to you.

It is quite common to find that once you learn your own Medicine you use less and less of it in wielding the forces of nature. The respect becomes so strong that you just do not call upon it. Learning first to work with the Elements themselves, the entities that dwell within them, and the spirits that rule there will allow understanding of what you are calling upon. If your requests are denied there is reason for that, whether or not you can see it. I urge caution only because if you consider the worst case scenario of each of the elemental forces—floods, earthquakes, volcanic eruptions, tornadoes—you will see that so much can go wrong. It only takes a small mistake to set things into motion, and once that motion is set it is very difficult to change. For this reason the shaman will rarely practice any Medicine unless it is absolutely necessary.

Shamanic Working

Shamanic work redirects the flow back to its natural form and includes the healing of mind, body, or spirit of an individual as well as works with the elemental forces that may be found askew. Most shamans can sense the working of a novice that has managed to fumble things. When there is magick in the air it can be felt or traced because it always leaves a residue recognized by seasoned practitioners. Begin by working on yourself, by healing yourself, purifying your path, and using the talents you were born with to fulfill basic needs. When you see that you can apply your skills to satisfy your needs, you will then see how you can apply them to the service of others.

Breaking Down Blockages

If our basic necessities in life are ignored, they weigh on the mind causing lack of focus. The trap occurs when you do not stop at the basic needs and become consumed with selfishness. You must know where to draw the fine distinguishing line. It is common to find these abilities naturally peeking through into your life as you begin your path, and yet the Gifts of Spirit can be blocked for years by fears or disbelief. You can block an entire concept because your parents told you as a child that you had an overactive imagination. It is common to have to rediscover them, and life does have a way of bringing the experiences back to be relearned. That is why your Guides are so important to your path. They will help you to reopen the doors. The truth is that you are made up of the same energies that you are tapping into, and the gifts themselves are a part of your very nature. The skills need to be honed and focused in positive directions so you can make good use of them.

When you focus on selfishness you become stuck, your skills are wasted, and you turn yourself into far less than you were meant to be. The rule of thumb is moderation, and that needs to be an issue at all times because power can become addictive. The thrill of first encountering a gift and the power it places in your hands is very tempting. Do not fall into the trap of thinking more is better. Ego must be contained, and if you see yourself as more important than others, wanting to swim in that power, you will find yourself drowning in it. The path you walk is sacred and should be honored as such. You were given life to serve and grow, not to control things.

Service to others has a positive effect on the lives around you and keeps you in balance. That which you put out returns with added force (for good or ill). Remembering to keep it positive will make it a rewarding experience. Those who receive many gifts are expected to use them in many ways and their responsibility is that much greater. As you journey and come into contact with Source Energy, sacred sites, and your own encounters with Spirit, you will discover that attitude is important. You were born to this life to learn and do specific work. You go to school and hold a job. Why not work on your spirit? Learning, no matter what form it takes, is a major part of life and we are all subject to it, or we hold ourselves back for another repeat lesson. Perhaps that is why the paths we walk seem so familiar to us at times. The familiarity, the rightness, the knowing of things you should not know by mundane standards all come into play. It is the call you are given to act or the pursuit of various things that has a spiritual ring to it, much like the tolling of a bell you once answered to, though now it only whispers.

A decision that leads to the progress or regression of your spirit must take place. It is what free will is all about. Obstacles are not there to stop you in your path and prevent success. They are there to make you stop to examine why they occurred in the first place. That examination, through journey work and questing, brings enlightenment and growth. If you are willing to face the challenges, then you will not take obstacles lying down or any other way. Sticking to a positive attitude brings the realization that your will controls your actions, and you need to let your inner spirit guide you in that control. Many people radiate a brilliant spirit. Conquering your fears, obstacles, and insecurities requires style, and you have to develop your own. It means fighting aspects of yourself in this process, but the battle resides within you, and journey work will help you to face it.

Giving and Receiving

If you say you cannot learn because of bad karma, or because you are not smart enough, or some other foolish reason, then you only serve to create yet another obstacle for yourself. Learning to forgive your past and learn from it is one of the major lessons. In the eyes of Spirit we are all worthy. The best way to deal with this is to open to Spirit and ask that your heart and spirit be washed clean of all the shadows and fears. You must be willing to give them up and to let them go.

Opening to Spirit in this manner brings a gentle cleansing with tenderness and generosity, teaching you the compassion you need to possess for yourself and for others. If you carry yourself as one who needs to know and is searching to find, you will discover a key to knowledge alongside the love you can give with it...the love and the wisdom to show it are what matters. You need to receive that love too. The greater the struggle, the greater the gift will be. You cannot hope to know everything, that is arrogant, but you do have the resources to all the answers for all the questions you can ask.

Spirit is like the Library of Congress and knows just what you need to hear. Like a library book, if you do not open it, you will never find the answers you are seeking. Be patient and gentle with yourself because there are bound to be some mistakes along the way. See them as learning experiences so growth may come quickly (usually accompanied by a rather deep and long sigh of being aware of your own blindness).

Stepping into your own sacred space, that of a Medicine Wheel, or entering a sacred site places you in the atmosphere of reception. While the flow of the energy itself will be felt internally by a woman, a man must tap it. That took me a long time to differentiate on my own. A woman needs to open to Source Energy by going within and to her natural rhythm, then releasing herself to it to let it flow outwardly. A man must look to the rhythm of the environment in which he finds himself, begin breathing with that rhythm and sending it alongside his inhaled breaths, then release himself to the flow. The difference is subtle, but it exists.

It is true that throughout nature, symbolism of masculine and feminine energies permeate all realms thoroughly in the positive, aggressive male and the negative, passive female. In this light that internal power may never be stripped unless we yield it up willingly. We need to share openly with a proper relationship of both male and female yielding up their mysteries to the other. This is not meant in a sexual context. It is internal for the female, thus natural to her. It is external for the male, thus something he must always be seeking...the passiveness and the aggression. When they are in balance all is right with the world, but you must learn to balance both natures within yourself as well. We are both female and male by nature, a paradox of truths that arises once again.

Mastering Your Gifts

It is not uncommon to need to repeat journeys for mastery of any gift or talent. Sometimes it comes all at once and enlightenment is like a bolt of lightning that allows understanding to dawn upon you. You simply know it is a truth and you see it for what it is. Physical manifestations, auditory voices, and visionary experiences all play a part either in conjunction with one another or separately. It is often a feeling of receiving an encyclopedia's worth of knowledge all at once. It makes sense to you and you understand it fully. It is on the return to the mundane world that the assimilation of this knowledge must take place and you must find a way to hone it. You may begin feeling overwhelmed by it all but the spirits that teach you on the journey will continue to oversee your progress. Intuitively you may sense a presence in your daily life or know when to journey again to reach your teachers. This cannot take place if you do not remain open to receiving their guidance. Trusting your instincts is critical to trusting yourself.

At the end of this chapter is a short exercise that I call the Smoking Mirror. It is designed to help you get in touch with your inner spirit and come to know it face to face. It provides a tangible path to its reality and a doorway to journey work that can be quite useful in various applications. It has been known to lead to shapeshifting experiences with Totems and can be used for that purpose as well. It is an exercise of the Western quadrant, the inner reflection of the Smoking Mirror that Bear presents when you enter hibernation within the womb. It is a soul-searching experience.

When you have a Dream Lodge experience in the mundane world you have to return and assimilate it, but the shift to the mundane has taken place automatically. Here, in this exercise, your interpretation must face the logical mind when you initially begin the work. It takes subconscious perception to see the true meaning of the symbolism and experience you will have. In either case, while in the Dream Lodge, or working with the Smoking Mirror, you have the ability to ask that things be explained in greater detail while they are happening. You can respectfully challenge issues to gain clarity but should not be surprised by how simple the answers seem to be. When looking for the overall perspective, always pull back your judgment to examine the entire picture, and then go in for the details.

Watch for the patterns to enlightenment. There is the lull that follows and allows for assimilation, then the period that allows you to hone and apply your skills. When they are mastered you are tested and can know that another lesson is soon to follow. The exception to this rule is when other lessons compliment the one you are being shown as a main focus. Then you may learn a few things simultaneously.

Wanting to share such experiences is quite common; using your gifts to teach will also come in time. Remember, however, that you cannot do these things until you have first served and healed yourself, learned the methods needed to wield such services, and to walk with Spirit as you do this. You can only teach and share what you know, you can only serve with honed skills, and you have to master these things in order to do that. The process of walking the path you are on is the process of spiritual growth. As you make progress the gifts will reveal themselves and you will begin setting new goals to keep you focused.

We will often discover that much more than achieving goals comes our way. When you reach the goals and turn back to see the road you have walked you will begin to realize this. You see the many gifts of Spirit, the progress, and come to know that each step you have taken has been right for you and always will be. We are all healers in one way or another. You have your own pace and gifts to serve you and those whose lives you touch. That is what makes you who you are and unique. Just as the paths of others will amaze you, the path you walk will amaze them. The assimilation process may mean that you step back from time to time to put things in order, but Spirit will always shed more light if it is needed. Sometimes it means taking one step forward and two back until you are ready to run. It is in knowing the gifts you possess and that what is right for you will come to you when the time calls for it...no sooner or later than that.

The Smoking Mirror

Begin by preparing your sacred space, and time this exercise for about a half hour from start to finish. Stand or seat yourself comfortably before a mirror to which a white candle has been lit on either side. Be certain the light of the candle allows your reflection to be clear but does not itself reflect in the surface of the mirror. I suggest white candles for the symbolism of purity, serenity, and truth.

Now with your index finger, trace a plus sign on the mirror right down the center of your nose and across the bridge between your eyes. Your finger will leave natural oils on the glass and give you a focal point to maintain a fixed gaze or hold onto images that may present themselves as the exercise progresses. It also serves to show you the surface of the mirror and define the space between you and the reflection you see.

Be certain all other lights are turned off before you begin. If you start to lose focus you need only to center your gaze on the crossed lines and back into your eyes to regain it. Gaze into your reflection looking straight into your eyes. When you are gazing into the mirror you want to lock onto the pupil of the eyes. Be sure you look deeply into them, not just at the eyes themselves. In the blackness of the center you will get your vision. It is like crystal-ball gazing to a degree. The vision takes place in the pupil and the size expands to encompass the vision as it comes. You can look into it or you can look at your reflected face and let the image shift to a Totem you need to focus on instead. This would depend on the purpose behind your work.

The face in the mirror will soon seem to be looking back at you and shift. The shift I am speaking of is one of distancing itself from you just slightly to the point of becoming that of a familiar stranger. When this takes place you will be looking into the eyes of your inner spirit and a conscious separation naturally takes place. Perceiving this other self as independent from you and allowing the truth to come through is important. Once you get the separation down you can meld again later when the trust is established and there can be some amazing journeys that take place this way.

At this point you may ask any questions of your Self that you wish and know the answers you receive will be truthful. Do not be surprised to discover that these answers may reveal issues and concepts that are much more than you originally thought they would be. You can focus on one question or any number of them and when you feel you are done you can turn on the lights, put out the candles, and wipe the mirror clean after giving thanks to Spirit. Go to your journal and make notes right away. This can be done as often as you like and it is a fantastic exercise to explore many things with...especially important decision making moments in your life. Whether you use this exercise to come to know your inner spirit or to become familiar with the ways of your Guides and their relative aspects to your own personality, it is a simple tool that will serve you well. Use it again and again. You will find with each encounter your skill level increases and the applications expand.

GLOSSARY

Above World: The realm of spiritual entities, Spirit, and higher consciousness.

Aindahing: The home within the heart where Great Mystery dwells and we are all one.

All Our Relations: All races and life forms.

Ally: A friendly spirit that often accompanies the Medicine Person throughout life.

Ancestors: Those who have passed over now serving Spirit in the role of Wisdom Keepers dwelling in the Below World.

Ancient Ones: Those of this world and others who have gone before us.

Animal Guides: Spirit animals that protect and guide the individual by teaching lessons in life.

Apport session: Gifts that are sent from the Spirit World dropping out of the air to physically materialize (jewelry, stones, coins, and other small items).

Bear Butte: A Native American sacred site in South Dakota.

Be Coming: The act of growing into what is already within you to be.

Below World: Realm of the Ancestors or Wisdom Keepers who serve Spirit.

Brujo: A sorcerer; generally of a dark path and negative works.

Centering: The act of finding your spiritual center amid the Seven Sacred Directions.

Ceremonial Highway: A Kings Road or processional way for coronation and royal events.

Ceremony: A set pattern of events to honor Spirit and other entities while experiencing union with them.

Channel: To open and become a vessel for Spirit, Guides, teachers, or spiritual entities to speak or act through.

Clairaudience: Literally, clear hearing.

Clairvoyance: Literally, clear sight.

Death Roads: Sometimes called "Ghost Roads" because many are said to be haunted. They are roadways that funeral processions follow to the grave site.

Divination: The art of foretelling future events, locating objects, or answering questions.

Dragon: An entity of the elemental realms as well as symbol of Fire.

Dream Lodge: The state of sleep where one experiences lucid dreams, spiritual dreams, or journeys to become practiced in the art of dreaming.

Drop robe: To leave the "robe," or physical body, behind as the inner spirit passes at death.

E S P: Extrasensory perception coming from heightened states of awareness through the senses.

Earth Lights: Phenomena that appear as drifting or dancing lights commonly found near sacred sites and vortexes.

Elder: An individual who has reached the age of 52 years; one who sits on a Council of Elders; those who have lived long enough to have experienced life sufficiently to advise others. They are all considered Elders. What they do with that title or role is their choice. It is not required of them, but it is an honor to be one no matter what choice is made. It is a title of wisdom gained in living life—like respect for a grandparent that may or may not choose to be in a position of authority.

Electric Vortex: A pool of energy spiraling upward and outward with the ability to charge any energy that comes into contact with it.

Equinox: Occurs in Spring and Fall when the periods of light and darkness are equal.

Feng-Shui: Chinese art of geomancy.

Firedrake: Fire Dragon dwelling in the flame.

Fire Sticks: Lightning.

Flying Buck: Shamanic symbol representing the flight of the spirit in shamanic journeys.

Four Winds: Sentient winds that preside over the four quarters of the world.

Geoglyph: Art that is laid out upon the land with rock, or shrubbery in large-scale design.

Geomancy: The study of the energy flows of the Earth for divination purposes.

Ghost Roads: *See* Death Roads.

Gifts of Spirit: Powers bestowed upon an individual by Spirit or spiritual entities on behalf of Spirit.

Give-Away: The time to give of yourself, your wisdom, your service to others that makes room for other blessings to be received.

Good Red Road: The path of the North-South axis of the Medicine Wheel.

Grandfather: Title of address showing respect to male spiritual entities and Elders.

Grandmother: Title of address showing respect to female spiritual entities and Elders.

Great Mystery: Source of the creative aspects and grand plan of the universe. A Native American term for the Creator, God, or Spirit.

Grounding: The act of releasing excess energy that follows all shamanic workings.

Guardian Spirit: A protective spirit entity that remains with an individual throughout life.

Holy Man: A Native American religious leader.

Impacting: A spiritual melding that is physically felt and generally initiated by the spirit. Can be a forced merger by the spirit.

Imprinting: Spiritual melding or merging that is done to last a lifetime and is generally initiated by the spirit itself where you merge as one.

Inner Wheel: The Medicine Wheel we carry within us when we live in harmony with life.

Kings Road: A road or processional way for ceremonial purpose.

Kiva: Wombs within Mother Earth built half above and half below the ground by the Anasazi to form ceremonial arenas; they marked locations where the Ancestors first emerged on land.

Land Temples: Formations of land that surround vortexes and Ley Lines creating a temple.

Ley Lines: Lines of energy that span Mother Earth in a webbed network channeling those energies of our planet and those of the universe itself.

Listening Stick: Held to remind others that it is time to listen and learn from one who speaks and teaches through oral tradition. It prevents interruption; used to teach or hold council.

Lucid Dream: A dream in which the dreamer is consciously aware of dreaming and gains the ability to take control to journey and work with Guides, Totem Animals, and teachers.

Magnetic Vortex: A pool of energy that spirals down and inward drawing to itself and grounding the energies it attracts.

Medicine Man: A shaman.

Medicine Wheel: A sacred circle used to create sacred space for rituals, ceremonies, and personal shamanic workings. It contains 36 stones, and is quartered with four sacred paths to the center, which is the Creator Stone. Each stone is a lesson of its own and together they hold the teachings of spiritual wisdom and spiritual Medicine, thus the name, Medicine Wheel.

Medicine Woman: A shamaness.

Meditation: The ability to still the chatter of the mind, focus on an issue, and receive enlightenment.

Merging: The act of bonded union between an individual and a spirit.

Middle World: The physical reality and center that create the Now or presence of the moment.

Moon Cycle: The menstrual cycle of a woman.

Moon Lodge: The place of dreaming, journey work, or spiritual isolation where a woman takes retreat during her menstrual cycle.

Namaji: Term used by the Ojibwa tribe meaning respect, honor, dignity, and pride.

Node: See vortex.

Now: The center of the moment you are in that includes past, present, and future. The core of time and no time.

Occult: The study of secret teachings beyond normal understanding.

Old Religion: Witchcraft and sometimes referring to paganism in general.

Other Side: Refers to the Spirit Worlds.

Otherworlds: Refers to realms of the spiritual dimensions.

Ouija Board: Sometimes called a "witch board." A board with letters and a planchette used to channel spirits, receive messages, or answer questions.

Out-of-body: Projection of the inner spirit.

Paranormal: Supernatural.

Pendulum: An item suspended from a length of string or a chain used for divination purposes.

Petroglyph: Rock art that is in the form of carving on stone.

Phoenix: Mythical bird that dies a flaming death only to arise from its own ashes. It is a symbol of the Element of Fire and the cycle of rebirth.

Pictograph: Rock art that is in the form of painted pictures.

Power Animal: A Totem spirit that complements an individual's personality traits and acts as a dominant spiritual guide or teacher. Generally highly protective of the individual to which they have attuned themselves.

Precognitive: Extrasensory perceptions that lead to premonitions or skills to foresee future events.

Projective Hand: The dominant hand most often used to do things—for working or for magickal purposes to send out the will.

Psychometry: The art of sensing things by handling objects and getting a reading from them.

Rainbow People: People of all races who walk with Spirit in balance, tolerance, and harmony.

Receptive Hand: The least dominant hand used to hold or receive. In magickal terms it is the hand that receives the energy of Spirit into the body.

Rite: A ritual ceremony used to mark a transition in the life of an individual.

Ritual: A set pattern of actions to bring about specific states of consciousness or events.

Rock Art: Pictures, designs, and patterns painted or carved on the surface of rocks; art that is laid out in rock formations on the surface of the land.

Runes: Ancient symbols used as methods of writing to mark a site, and as wards of protection, to bring good luck, or cast in the practice of divination.

Sacred Space: A focused and safe working environment on both physical and spiritual levels that permeates all dimensions.

Seance: Individuals gathered together within a circle, hand to hand, to contact the Spirit World. The group is generally led by someone with the ability to act as a medium or channel.

Seven Sacred Directions: East and the Element of Air; South and the Element of Fire; West and the Element of Water; North and the Element of Earth; the Above, Middle, and Below Worlds.

Shadow Nature: The darker side of our personality or self that we hide from others or struggle with.

Shaman: A spiritual wise person, leader, healer, Medicine Person that can be either male or female (referred to as a shamaness).

Shamanic Flight: Projection of the inner spirit into the physical as well as dimensional realms.

Shamanic Journey: A state of trance allowing the individual to enter into spiritual realms and dimensions. This is done internally or by projecting either the mind or the inner spirit out of the body to explore, heal, or receive lessons.

Shamanic Tree: A tree symbolizing the Above, Middle, and Below Worlds of the shaman and the centering among the Elements.

Shapeshifting: The ability to become one, or transform the inner spirit into the essence of another creature or life form. This allows the individual to move and perceive through that essence consciously or be guided by it.

Sipapu: A sacred location or point of exit and entry into this world and beyond. Locations where the Ancestors emerged onto the surface of the land and life originated.

Sky People: Entities of the higher spiritual realms such as Guides, teachers, angels, and so forth.

Smoking Mirror: The inner reflection of the self in the mind's eye.

Solstice: In Summer, it is the longest day of the year and turning point to longer nights. In the Winter, it is the longest night of the year and turning point to longer days.

Source Energy: A term I coined representing the energy coming from Spirit and the universe and permeating all that exists. This energy can be tapped and channeled to influence the effects of the work done on the Medicine Path.

Spirit: Native American term for the Creator, God, or Supreme Being if presented with a capital "S." A lowercase "s" represents an entity in non-physical form.

Spirit Guide: A spiritual entity that guides and teaches an individual through the spirit realms or channels information to them from other dimensions.

Spirit Keeper: The animal essence of a spirit that keeps the mysteries of an element in service to Spirit and Great Mystery.

Spirit of Place: Spiritual entity dwelling at a specific location; generally at a sacred site. Sentient energy.

Spirit Roads: Physical roadways for sacred, ritual, or ceremonial purposes. Religious rites such as initiations often take place along them as well as the reenactment of sacred myths.

Spiritualism: Religious or paranormal teachings and methods of contacting spirits of the deceased and other realms. Generally it is focused on the spirits of family, friends, or renowned individuals.

Standing People: The spirits of trees.

Stone People: The spirits of rocks.

Tap Walk: A term I coined to express taking a walk in nature and tapping into the energies of the area, the Voice of the Land, and any spirits that may reside locally.

Tarot: Cards used as sacred tools and read for divination purposes.

Telepathy: Thought transference.

Thunder Beings: Powerful spirits of Air and storms.

Tobacco Ties: Small pouches of tobacco used as spiritual offerings.

Totem Animal: The animal essence or spirit that reflects aspects of an individual's nature. They can act as Guides, protectors, and teachers. Totem Animals remain with the individual for life and can be as few as one or numerous.

Trance: Varying degrees of altered consciousness and spiritual awareness.

Veil of Illusion: The mundane or physical world and consciousness.

Vision Quest: A ceremonial procedure that allows an individual to receive a vision from Spirit that will influence his or her life and the lives of others profoundly.

Voice of the Land: Attunement with nature at a given location where communication can take place and the individual is able to speak with the land or other living aspects of it.

Vortex: A location of condensed energies that whirlpool in either an upward or downward manner, which affects all energies coming into contact with it. Generally found where two or more Ley Lines cross.

Web of Life: That which connects us all through Spirit.

White Buffalo Calf Woman: A spirit woman of prophecy from the Sioux Indians.

Will-O-the-Wisps: Phenomena that appear as drifting or dancing lights.

Yang: Chinese term for negative or feminine energy.

Yin: Chinese terms for positive or masculine energy.

SELECTED BIBLIOGRAPHY

Black Elk, Wallace, and William S. Lyon, *Black Elk: The Sacred Ways of a Lakota*. New York: HarperCollins Publishers, 1990.

Brown, Joseph Epes. *The Sacred Pipe*. Norman: University of Oklahoma Press, Norman Publishing, 1953.

Devereux, Paul. *Places of Power*. New York: Sterling Publishing Company, Inc., 1990.

Devereux, Paul. *Shamanism and the Mystery Lines*. St. Paul: Llewellyn Publications, 1994.

Lame Deer, John (Fire), and Richard Erdoes, *Lame Deer: Seeker of Visions*. New York: Simon and Schuster, Inc., 1972.

Lee, Scout Cloud. *The Circle Is Sacred: A Medicine Book for Women*. Tulsa: Council Oak Books, 1998.

Neihardt, John G. *Black Elk Speaks*. Lincoln: University of Nebraska Press, 1932.

Mails, Thomas E. *Fools Crow*. Lincoln: University of Nebraska Press, 1979.

Mails, Thomas E. *Fools Crow: Wisdom and Power.* Tulsa: Council Oak Books, 1991.

Mann, Nicholas R. *Sedona: Sacred Earth.* Albuquerque: Ziva Publishers, 1989.

Sams, Jamie. *The 13 Original Clan Mothers.* New York: HarperCollins Publishers, 1994.

Storm, Hyemeyohsts. *Seven Arrows.* New York: Ballantine, 1972.

Sun Bear, Wabun Wind, and Crysalis Mulligan. *Dancing with the Wheel: TheMedicine Wheel Workbook.* New York: Simon and Schuster, 1991.

INDEX

ABOUT THE AUTHOR

Cinnamon Moon has been a practicing Medicine Woman for more than 35 years, with a foundation in the tradition of the Lakota Sioux. Being an eclectic student of Native American Spirituality, her teachings include those of other Indian Nations as well. Ordained in the Universal Life Church, Cinnamon ministers to the needs of those who come to her on a private basis. Her counseling includes working with individuals and their families for those who are about to pass over into the realm of Spirit. Having taught Native American Spirituality for the past 25 years, she and close friends have created a Web site (*spiritlodge.org*) where they take a non-profit approach to spiritual teachings and networking. Being a Medicine Woman is a way of life for her as she strives to promote tolerance for all faiths, cultures, and races of humanity. Her goal is to help foster the vanishing lines of division between cultural traditions and encourage harmony among All Our Relations. Knowing the Medicine Path well, Cinnamon is dedicated to the service of Spirit through her pathwork, ministry, and writing.